Mapping an Understanding

Copyright © 2025 by Lloyd Hawkeye Robertson and Teela Roberston
Cover Design by Lianne Torres Barraquio 2025

All rights reserved. No part of this book may be reproduced in any manner whatsoever without written permission except in the case of brief quotations embodied in critical articles and reviews. No part of this book may be used to train LLMs or any form of AI. Pete's Press and its imprints exclusively publish works by human creatives and artists.
First Printing, 2025 by Pete's Press.
The Penny University Press is an imprint of Pete's Press.

Mapping an Understanding

How to visually represent the self in psychotherapy and research

Lloyd Hawkeye Robertson and
Teela Robertson

CONTENTS

TABLE OF CONTENTS vii

1. Introduction - Summary of Research — 1
2. Starting the Map — 9
3. An Initial Cognitive Self-map — 16
4. Creating a Self-Map using the Narrative Approach — 27
5. Using Self-mapping to Effect Change — 41
6. Understanding Transition and Non-Transition — 54
7. Working with Clients from Collectivist Cultures — 72
8. Creating Representational Visual Images — 87
9. Limitations and Concluding Thoughts — 90

APPENDIX A 92
APPENDIX B 96
HANDOUTS 102
REFERENCES 108
ABOUT THE AUTHORS 113

Sections

1. **Introduction- Summary of research, intended use, and theory**

   What are memes and how do they exert forces of attraction?
   The Self as a Complex of Memes
   The Potential of Memetic Mapping for Understanding the Self

2. **Starting the Map: Two ways to gather individual identifying data**

   Is it a meme?
   A detailed look at the two methods of meme identification

3. **An initial cognitive self-map using the "Forty Persons" method**

   Identifying and Placing Memes in Suzie's Self
   Reconstructing the Self: Reframing and Modifying Memes
   What schools of psychotherapy could utilize self-mapping?

4. **Creating a Self-Map using the Narrative approach**

   Using the Narrative approach: An Example
   Recognizing Complexity in Building upon the Basic Self-Map
   The Complex Self-Map as a Small World Network

5. **Using Self-mapping to Effect Change**

   Reflections on Maps of the Self
   Seven Core Elements of the Modern Self
   Empowerment and Self-Efficacy

6. **Understanding Transition and Non-transition in Self Development**

   Examples of Transitioning Selves
   The False Self and Mini-selves

      A Transsexual Self
      Revising client self-maps

7. **Working with Clients from Collectivist Cultures**

      Working with the Indigenous Self
      The Appeal of Collectivism
      Religion and popular culture

8. **Creating Representational Visual Images of the Self**
9. **Limitations and Concluding Thoughts**

Appendix A: A Sample of how Text was Segmented and Coded for the Meme
Appendix B: The Memes Used in Building Tina's Self Showing Referent
Appendix C: Handouts
References

About the Authors

1

Introduction - Summary of Research

Intended Use, and Theory

The purpose of this manual is to guide psychologists, counsellors, social workers, and other therapists in preparing maps of the self that they can use with their clients for the purpose of increasing self-understanding and therapeutic planning. This is a companion manual to *The Evolved Self*: Mapping an Understanding of Who We Are (2020) that describes a healthy or functional self composed of seven fundamental elements. We hope this manual will prove useful in assisting practitioners in a technique to better understand their clients, but more fundamentally, to aid the clients in better understanding themselves. It is our experience that when clients see themselves represented in map form and when those maps resonate with their sense of being, they will spontaneously engage in a process of self-change and that change is fundamental to the practice of counselling and psychotherapy (Dryden et al., 2001; Rodebaugh & Chambless, 2004; Wampold, 2000).

The self, as used here, is core to such concepts as self-esteem (De Man & Gutierrez, 2002), self-actualization (McAdams, 2012), and self-efficacy (Lightsey et al., 2014). That core is not entirely coterminous with conscious identity, as it involves unconscious, often inherited drives and dispositions. We evolved the ability to identify and solve problems; and, as Gazzaniga (2000) observed, a being that can get productive answers to its questions "cannot help but give birth to the concept of self. Surely one question the device would ask is, 'Who is solving all these problems? Let's call it *me*'- and away it goes!" (p. 1320). While we are not always conscious of that which drives us, we have the potential to become so.

Suffixes such as esteem, actualization, and efficacy added to the self are descriptors of how competent the organism perceives itself to be in responding to problems. The self-esteem movement of the 1980s confused correlation with causation, leading to the misleading and sometimes damaging slogan "You can become whatever you want to be." While it seems plausible that we need to believe we can do something in order to aspire to do it, raising self-esteem does not foster increased academic or occupational competence (Baumeister et al., 2004). Indeed, higher mathematical self-esteem among students in the United States is associated with lower achievement when compared to Chinese students (Wang & Lin, 2008). Ideally, self-construal should be reality-based, and include an accurate appraisal of one's abilities and achievements. One of the most effective means of effecting change in the self is to present evidencerr, congruent with the client's view of what constitutes evidence, that a previous self-construal was inaccurate. The ability to change one's worldview and one's self at the core of that worldview was a recent development in human history.

The self is often presented as a cognitivist project of self-definition, and while that level of consciousness now forms part of our definition as a species, elements that make up the self have been evolving for hundreds of thousands of years. To understand the self, we need to take into account that which is primordial.

Referencing western philosophy, major schools of psychology, cross-cultural experience, and qualitative research involving self-mapping, *The Evolved Self* developed an argument that a "modern self" capable of individual volitional planning is a cultural artifact that evolved prior to the "Axial Age" (Jaspers, 1951; Mahoney, 1991; Robertson 2017a) when most of the great religions of the world came into being. These religious movements, along with some modern ideologies are concerned with maintaining a collective identity thus regulating or diminishing qualities of individuality that could challenge the collectivity. We support a hypothesis that a healthy or functional self in all cultures is composed of both collectivist and individualist elements, including constancy, individual volition, uniqueness, productivity, intimacy, remembering or reflecting, emotion, and social interest. The self then includes that which is genetically inheritable, interpreted, or supplemented with that which may be culturally learned. The interplay of genetic, cultural, and personal experience that contributes to an implicit self is represented in Figure 1.

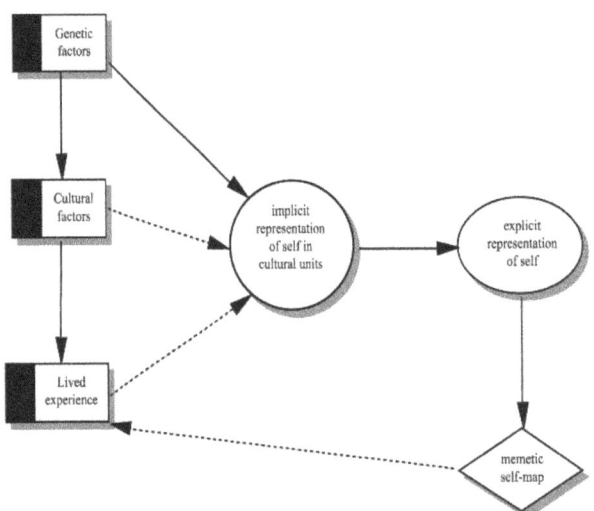

Figure 1: A representation of the conceptual framework showing the interplay of cultural and environmental factors leading to a representation of the self that can be mapped.

As can be interpolated from Figure 1, the implicit self that exists in most of us is made explicit in counselling and is then mapped using elemental cultural units or memes set in relation to each other. Having a self allows one to take oneself as an object. Such a self may then be situated in past events in a process of reflection, or in possible futures allowing for prediction and planning. While we are largely determined by genetic and environmental programming, this ability to situate ourselves in past and future events allows us a modicum of free will; in effect, we have the ability to reprogram ourselves (Robertson, 2017a).

While Paleolithic peoples had cultures that included Stone Age tools, representational painting, and burials, thus indicating a form of self around 50,000 BCE, there is no indication that they had developed the ability to take their individual selves as an object. While it is conceivable that a person could learn a technique of doing so without a modicum of language, the development of indexical pronouns in Greek and Egyptian cultures around 1,000 BCE allowed this skill, necessary for objective thought, to be transmitted through language (Jaynes, 1976; Johnson, 2003). Normally, selves are individually held with one self attached to one body; and the self, with a similar structure, is found in both individualist and collectivist cultures (Robertson, 2020). The difference between individualist and collectivist cultures is one of emphasis—individualist cultures proclaim that the individualism already inherent within the self is good.

Culture provides a menu from which such an objective self can be constructed, and the building blocks for such construction are elemental units of culture that, in this manual, we call "memes." The short definition of "meme" is the smallest unit of culture that is self-replicating (Dawkins, 1976), but as we shall see, the definition that is useful when considering the self must be more elaborate, taking into account that which mimics forces of attraction and repulsion between memes.

What are memes and how do they exert forces of attraction?

Some units of culture are better remembered than others. Conversely, some true statements may be resistant to belief. For example, soon after the turn of the millennium, one of the authors (LHR) gave a group of university health undergrads the following true and false question on an exam: "The majority of Acquired Immune Deficiency (AIDS) cases are in Africa (true or false)." Every student marked the column for "false," even though the answer was true by a significant margin. This would be an example of a repellent meme. We can speculate that a disproportionate amount of attention given to the pandemic in North America, the emphasis given to "safer" sex (with the implication that only abstinence led to actual safety), and a notion of political correctness that identifying people with black or dark skin with a negative outcome was racist had the effect of repelling the idea that the majority of AIDS cases are in Africa. At the level of affect, the right answer to the exam question did not feel right. In this example we can see concretely how connotation and affect led to a behaviour (denial) as an outcome.

Atran (2002) compared normal subjects with those who have autism by asking samples from each group to interpret ideological and religious sayings such as "Let a thousand flowers bloom" and "To everything there is a season." Autistic subjects showed a significant tendency to closely paraphrase and repeat content from the original statement (for example, "Don't cut flowers before they bloom"). The non-autistic controls tended to infer a wider range of cultural meanings with little replicated content (for example: "Go with the flow" or "Everyone should have equal opportunity"). The non-autistic subjects were engaging in inference, not unlike the university students faced with the previous question about AIDS. But there was no true or correct inference. While the autistic subjects were good replicators of the memes they were given, the non-autistic subjects went in different directions with their answers. It can be said, therefore, that the non-autistic subjects were interpretively individualizing the memes that they were presented with the implication that for them, the mechanism by which memes replicate does not exist external to the individual.

Equating memes with urban legends, Heath, Bell, & Sternberg (2001) studied the effect of emotional valence on meme propagation. A series of three experiments using university undergraduates determined that stories evoking reactions of interest, disgust, and surprise were more likely to be passed on with the emotion of disgust the most powerful motivator irrespective of the story's plausibility. Emotion, forming part of the replicating unit, mimics forces of attraction and repulsion between memes. Emotional valence has been identified in the spread of memes as a social contagion (Mazambani et al., 2015).

Defining the term 'meme' as a unit of cultural transmission containing a specific substantive message, Robles-Diaz-de-Leon (2003) used different strategies to produce environmentally friendly behaviour in five Mexican villages. In three of the villages, she used traditional strategies for dealing with environmental problems such as town hall meetings to discuss the problem and publicity in the form of posters to direct behaviour (for example, clean up the garbage). In two of the towns she created a meme, which she called the "Limpio meme" (Robles-Diaz-de-Leon, 2003, p. 88) that included a positive emotive goal (for example, we want a clean community), a problem statement (for example, we need to reduce wastewater or garbage in the streets), a behavioural injunction (for example, "You need to put wastewater at the town disposal site, or you need to pick up garbage to clean the streets), an appeal to social interest ("We know everything is better when we work together), and a directive to spread the meme ("Tell others about this plan"). She then measured the effectiveness of each strategy by measuring the changes in environmental conditions over a four-month period. She found that the villages where a memetic approach was used were most effective in inducing the villagers to engage in environmentally friendly behaviours, and it mattered not whether the memes so used were co-constructed in village meetings or whether she created the meme herself and put up posters containing each of the elements listed above. In contrast, those villages in which town hall meetings were called to discuss the problems or where posters were put up directing villagers to engage in environmentally friendly behaviours fared less well, and in some cases behaviours regressed into less environmentally friendly acts.

The constructed "Limpio" (clean) memes were smaller than an urban legend but larger than a word or simple concept containing a number of concepts linked by connotative, emotive and behavioural factors. Robles-Diaz-de-Leon concluded that the most successful method of aiding people to change their behaviours involved the use of memes with no difference recorded between the effectiveness of the meme developed through participatory co-construction or researcher construction alone.

The studies on urban legends and environmental activism suggest connotation and affect as the source of such attraction, which, added to Dawkins' (1976) originating concept, results in the following definition: A meme is the smallest unit of culture having referent, connotative, affective, and behavioural components that may be transmitted from one person to another. Such a meme would rarely, if ever, be copied in its entirety from one mind to another. While memes exist outside of the individual within the universe of culture, they exhibit no necessary valence in that state. For that we need individual consciousness which involves the active construction of maps of reality (Seth, 2021).

The arrows in Figure 2 represent how units of culture or memes flow between levels of culture. Initially, infants receive their culture from their family or other caregivers, who attribute their emotional displays to cause and motivation. In this process infants begin to develop ideas as to who they are and how they fit into the world. Later they begin to absorb ideas from their community with memes that fit with who they already are and how they have been taught to interpret the world more readily absorbed than other memes. Later, they become influenced by the larger society through media, educational institutions, business, and government organizations, but in fact, those influences have already been mediated by family. Since culture is a collective mind with the individual influencing its direction by promoting some ideas and not others. The individual is both created by and is the creator of culture.

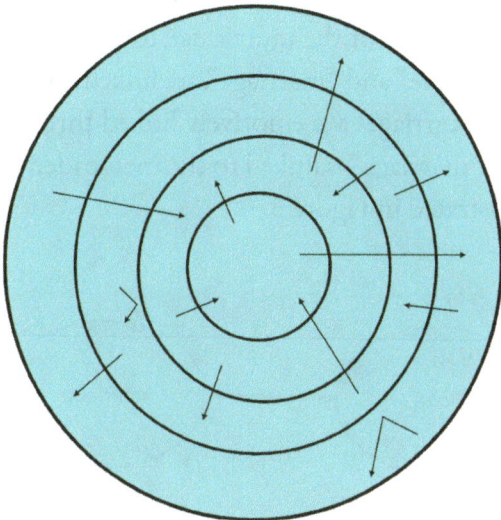

Figure 2: The self nested in family, community and macro-societal cultures

All major psychotherapies start from the premise of the client as an individual with unique experiences, interpretations, and social relations. Clients are empowered to make changes to their selves in keeping with their experiences, and we propose self-mapping as a way of making their implicit selves explicit. We start by conceptualizing the self as a complex arrangement of cultural memes.

The Self as a Complex of Memes

While Susan Blackmore (1999) first suggested that the self is a complex of memes, she failed to suggest a way of identifying and ordering them. It had been generally understood that the self was a cultural construct (Blustein & Noumair, 1996; Mead, 1912/1990; Shotter, 1997) that appeared to change dependent on context (Battaglia, 1995; Neimeyer, 2002) while imparting a sense that the same person exists over time (Damon & Hart, 1988; Louisy, 1996; Tippett et al., 2018). Dawkins' (1976) had said memes exhibit attractive and repellent properties. Such properties, if they could be demonstrated, would allow clusters of memes to form within minds with a degree of temporal fidelity and fecundity. The resultant formation would be both stable and variable and it would be possible to represent such units within those clusters graphically. It was necessary to define those units before they could be mapped in relation to each other.

Memes had previously been described as having cognitive and behavioural dimensions (Csikszentmihalyi, 1993; Dawkins, 1986; Robles-Diaz-de-Leon, 2003), with the cognitive dimension including an accepted meaning accompanied by associated connotations. Behaviour associated with a meme serves a replicative function within a given culture while reinforcing the individual's commitment to the meme in question. Emotions also play a role in maintaining the self (Damasio, 1999; Donald, 2001; Leary & Tangney, 2003), and emotional valence has been identified with respect to memes in urban legends (Heath et al., 2001) and negative reciprocity (Freidman & Sing, 2004). Flowing from this, a meme is defined as a unit of culture that exhibits referent, connotative, affective, and behavioural properties.

Such memes could be linked associatively by connotation and affect, thus mimicking forces of attraction. For example, if, in the mind of the individual, love and marriage go together like a horse and carriage, then in that mind, "love" and "marriage" are linked connotatively, as are horses and carriages. Further, if marriages and carriages are emotively linked through association, then the meme identified by the referent word "marriage" is linked to the meme identified by the referent word "carriage." This relationship is illustrated in Figure 3.

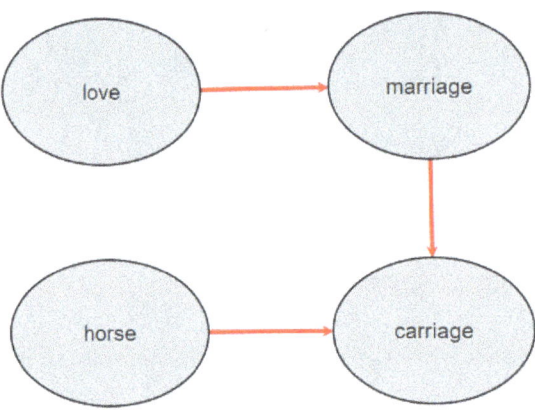

Figure 3: A graphic illustration of love, marriage, horse and carriage where marriage has an emotional association with carriages

Dawkins (1976) said complexes of memes built through attraction as illustrated in Figure 3 come to predominate within a 'cultural soup' dependent, not on their utility to their human hosts, but on their replicative ability. Mutations could bring unexpected results: "Scholars of the Septuagint started something big when they mistranslated the Hebrew word for 'young woman' into the Greek word for 'virgin,' thereby coming up with a prophecy, 'Behold, a virgin shall conceive and bear a son" (p. 18). In response to the resultant implication of cultural determinism, Steven Pinker (1997) replied, "A complex meme does not arise from the retention of copying errors. It arises because some person knuckles down, racks his brain, musters his ingenuity, and composes or writes or paints or invents something" (p. 209). In fairness to Dawkins, he had previously stated, "We have the power to defy the selfish genes of our birth and, if necessary, the selfish memes of our indoctrination" (1976, p. 215), implying just the sort of process described by Pinker. To the extent that memes control our thoughts and behaviours we are subject to cultural determinism; however, if we can create new memes as suggested by Pinker or differentially select memes according to our fancy, then we are exercising at least a modicum of free will.

To summarize, a meme is a small unit of culture with distinctive properties that mimic the forces of attraction and repulsion. Memes can come to us through a process of cultural determinism (Coyne, 2012; Robertson, 2017b), but we can create new memes or reorder existing memes in new ways. Thus, we both create and are created by culture, and that which is "us" can be mapped in resultant units of culture.

Factors that are often not consciously understood by the individual include genetic predispositions, habitual emotions, hormonal change, or environmental variables that influence perception and trigger particular sequences of behaviours. Strictly speaking, we cannot map that of which we are not conscious, yet such non-cognitive factors can activate particular sequences or aspects within the self in a way that defies linear sequential thinking. It is proposed that self-map efficacy may be enhanced with the inclusion of psychological characteristics and that situating them in conscious awareness can aid collaborative therapeutic planning. Linked memes show pathways of thought associated with one's self-identity. The use of memetic self-maps as outlines of overarching, grammatically based meta-narratives is explored. This manual offers guidance in the use and mapping of such factors.

The Potential of Memetic Mapping for Understanding the Self

This manual serves to provide a deep understanding of the concepts and application of memetic mapping so therapists can successfully engage clients in the process. We explore the two methods for developing maps; one tends to have the best practical application for therapy, and the other method is best for research. This difference is predominantly based on the time available while actively engaging in therapy versus a research study. Once we describe key concepts and the process involved, we incorporate background information to facilitate understanding of how memetic mapping has been applied to date and to illustrate the process by which maps are developed.

The information described here builds off *The Evolved Self* (2020), which focused on research of the cross-cultural utility of self-mapping. We work to clarify and describe self-mapping and its therapeutic uses to the best of our ability given the influence of the individual characteristics and style of each client and therapist. Memetic mapping is broken down into a step-by-step process to develop a map with which the client identifies.

The goal of the therapist is to co-construct a map of the self that resonates with the client. "Resonation" is defined here as the cognitive recognition that the graphic representation does, in fact, represent the individual coupled with the feeling that it succeeds in some essential ways. The verbal response to such identification might be "That's me!" Once a client resonates with their map, there are many directions a therapist can go. In this manual, we identify key components that should be present in a self-map, as well as patterns therapists may identify that can be worked on to increase a client's understanding of their self or to enact change, as well as further considerations. Our recent experience of using the mapping process in therapy (Robertson & Robertson, 2024) supports the suggestion of psychotherapeutic benefits experienced by participants and clients as described in *"The Evolved Self"* (2020, pp. 228-28):

1) Preparing the self-maps recognized the participant as an expert in him or herself, thus helping establish a collaborative equality;

2) Rapport is developed quickly to the extent that often by the second interview, participants are willing to share sensitive details about their personal lives they had initially avoided;

3) The act of participating in the map-making exercise reminds participants of prior interpretive choices made in response to transitional experiences with the implication they can make other choices;

4) Memetic self-map co-construction often increases a sense of empowerment or control over one's being;

5) The visual representation of the self allowed the psychologist and participant in research or therapy to place contemplated changes in perspective with respect to the entire self;

6) The absence of items identified as common to selves (continuity, volition, individuation, productivity, intimacy, social interest, feeling) may be "red-flagged" by the therapist for further examination; and,

7) Recognition of attractive forces existent between individual memes and the placement of memes with respect to other memes may precursor the development of effective strategies for self-change.

In this manual, we describe two ways of creating self-maps, case studies involving the use of these maps, the use of self-mapping with minority populations, and the use of self-mapping software. It is recommended that the reader keep the potential benefits listed here in mind as you read the rest of this manual.

2

Starting the Map

Two ways to gather individual identifying data

Do you want quick clinical results or are you more research-oriented? This question highlights the distinction between the two approaches used to identify personal self-defining memes in this manual. The "quick" approach was initially developed to assist a suicidal youth who is described in Chapter 3. It is a directive approach asking the client to complete and rank order the following four lists:

1. Ten persons they are (defining roles),
2. Ten things they believe to be true (core beliefs),
3. Ten things they like about themselves (positive attributes), and
4. Ten things they would change about themselves if they could (negative attributes).

It is a best practice to present the four task lists and let the clients start answering on their own before offering prompts. In practice, most clients are quick to identify the ten persons they are. Prompts may be given to have them explore the different hats they wear in life and the roles they fill in the family, communities, and institutions they occupy. In my practice (TJR), clients most often struggle with identifying ten things they believe to be true. This question requires deeper reflection on the beliefs and principles that guide their lives and decisions. To support this, therapists should listen between the lines in the history the client provides and uncover what they value and what beliefs underlie those. Responses may reflect beliefs they have about what they expect from themselves and the world, culture, religion, the capacities of people, and how things ought to be. The ten things they like about themselves and ten things they would change if they could tend to be more straightforward. Clients who are not deep thinkers or are preoccupied by the material world may start to focus on physical attributes; these are often not memes depending on the meaning to the person. Clients may need to be reminded to consider their perceived strengths and weaknesses in various life domains. Things they would change about themselves don't have to be realistic. Sometimes things they can't change, like having diabetes, may have a powerful effect on how they live and perceive themselves. This could also extend to family of origin issues, attributes, and mental health struggles they might not believe they can be free of. When we are struggling to give a referent title to an idea on the list, I find it helpful to ask, "What *does this say about you as a person?*" This often triggers a meaningful word rooted in a belief about their selfhood.

The therapist then reviews each list to determine which represent memes using the definition that memes must have a referent name and cognitive, emotive, and behavioural elements or implications. Items are rank ordered from easiest to hardest to change or give up, with those that are ranked higher held to be more central to the core of the client's self. Duplicate items are deemed to be of increased import and therefore more central to the person's being than indicated by the initial ranking. The potential weakness of this method is that there could be components of the self that do not lend themselves to being on one of these four lists. Therapists must consider the initial interview and stories offered by clients during the process.

In contrast, the narrative method, illustrated in Chapter 4, begins with the client answering, in detail, the question "Who are you?" supplemented by exemplars, anecdotes, and desires. The clinician then transcribes and segments the narrative, putting labels on each segment representing the content of that segment. Segments with the same label are placed in the same bin with the number of segments in each bin. The contents of each bin are examined to see if the combined qualities are sufficient to represent a meme. The "strength" of each meme is taken from the number of segments that meme was repeated in the narrative. While this method appears to be less directive, it is dependent on the focus of the client, with the result that some aspects could be missed. The therapist must be prepared to shift the client's focus to ensure all aspects of his or her self are covered. Before using either method, the therapist needs to have a solid grounding on what constitutes a meme.

Is it a meme?

A meme is the smallest unit of culture that is self-replicating. It is more complex than a simple idea that is not in itself emotively or behaviorally charged. Similarly, it is not simply a concept, although some concepts could be memes, nor is it a synonym for the word "word." For example, the adjective in the phrase "the red apple" is not a meme but the term "red" as applied to a political movement might be.

Practitioners creating self-maps need to ensure that only properly defined memes are mapped as such. Memes "speak" to the individual in a way that most words and concepts do not. As we saw in Chapter 1, memes infer connotative meaning that is, perhaps, unique to the individual, and this allows individuals with the same referent or "dictionary definition" of a meme to impute different understandings. A meme is not, therefore, a static entity that can be captured in its entirety by definition, but a "moving target" with direction. By understanding the connotation attached to the referent, the therapist can understand the meme's direction for the individual. That direction will be accompanied by emotional valence; emotions such as fear, love, hope, concern, anxiety, curiosity, or disgust attached to the meme not only give the meme significance, it leads to action. The "Limpio" meme (Robles-Diaz-de-Leon, 2003, p. 88) described earlier in Chapter 1 contained two behavioural directives: 1) to engage in specific environmentally friendly behaviours and 2) to pass the meme on to others. To be successful, memes need only replicate, and while referent meanings can be stored in books and computers outside of the self, the connotative, emotive, and behavioural aspects that allow for replication are within the individual. Thus, when working with clients, the task of the therapist is to identify the referent, connotative, emotive, and behavioural components that constitute each meme. If a concept, idea, or word does not have these four components, it is not a meme.

We agree with Burman (2012) that the meme as a replicator cannot exist separately from its medium of replication. Each meme is individualized with the provision that the holder of the meme likely believes that his or her associated connotative, emotive, and behavioural associations are in some sense "correct" and may attempt to promote such "correctness" to others. It is not our role as therapists to assess the correctness of meme structure but to attempt to understand individualized memes in their fullness and to record how memes attract or repel other memes to form the structure we call the self. The forces of attraction that lead to the creation of the self are the connotative, emotive, and behavioural elements attached to the referent word or concept that labels the meme. As we saw with the manually constructed "Limpio" meme, connotative and emotive factors drive behaviours that contribute to (or inhibit) memetic propagation. Further, the forces of attraction between memes give the self the stability that allows us to say that the "me" that I observe today is the same person that was "me" last year.

A detailed look at the two methods of meme identification

We commend two methods that can be used to identify specific memes when preparing maps of the self. These two, the "Forty Persons" and the "Narrative" methods, each have strengths, which are discussed here. The Forty Persons method used in the case study found in Chapter 3 is more directive, involving the following steps:

1. The subject creates 4 lists of 10 or more self-descriptors each. The four lists include "persons I am," "things I believe to be true," "things I would change about myself if I could," and "things I like about myself;"
2. The items on each list are prioritized from 1 to 10. One way of prioritizing each list would be to ask the subject which of the ten items would be easiest to discard or remove from who they are. That item or belief becomes item 10. What could be discarded next would become item 9, and so on;
3. Each item is given a referent word or phrase reflecting a self-statement. For example, the statement, "I would lose weight," on the list containing ten things the subject or client would change about himself or herself might, in consultation, be coded "heavy," "overweight," or "big;"
4. Referents of the same meme from different lists are combined if the client's meaning for each is the same or closely matches;
5. Referent words representing concepts that contain affective, connotative, and behavioral dimensions are declared to be memes. It is important to explore these dimensions of the meme with the client prior to its inclusion in the self-map;
6. Those memes that were given higher priority are given centrality when preparing the self-map.

7. Memes that share affective, connotative or behavioral dimensions are linked with connecting edges;
8. Memes that are more strongly associated with another meme are placed in close proximity to that meme;
9. Memes that are repellant or in opposition to each other are drawn with a field of force showing repulsion.

The narrative method, which we also commend, is less directive and was used in our initial qualitative study into the structure of the self. The client or research participant (dependent on context) is asked to describe, in detail, who they are, and this description is recorded. Typically, people will tend to focus on a limited number of aspects of themselves dependent on context, expectations, and priming. The therapist should be prepared with supplementary questions such as the following to ensure a full and complete self-description:

1. How would you describe yourself to explain who you are?
2. What are you like/not like?
3. What kind of person are you?
4. What are you especially proud of about yourself?
5. How did you get to be the way you are?
6. What major events happened that led to changes in who you are?
7. If you change from year to year, how do you know it's the same you?
8. What makes you a unique person, distinct from others?
9. What gives you a sense of meaning or purpose?

Once the therapist and client agree that a full and rich description has been recorded, the narrative is then transcribed and coded for items meeting our definition of memes. Specifically, the transcript is segmented into phrases with each phrase representing a single thought. Each segment is coded with a referent word representing the content of that thought. All the phrases representing units of thought with the same referent are placed together in the same "bin" and the content of each bin is reviewed for evidence of connotative, affective, and behavioural meaning. Those referents with these three components are declared to be memes, with those memes that are cited most often in the transcript declared to be more central to the self for mapping purposes. As with the "Forty Persons" method, memes sharing connotative, affective, or behavioural properties are considered to be linked. The steps in the self-narrative method can be listed as including:

1. The client is asked to describe who he or she is using prompts to ensure a rich description;
2. The resultant narrative is transcribed and segmented according to units of thought. A unit of thought conveys a single idea or description;
3. Each segment is given a referent code word;
4. All segments with the same referent code are placed in the same "bin" or grouped together for comparison.

5. Bins with the same code word exhibiting connotative, affective, and behavioral dimensions are declared to be memes.
6. Memes with more representative segments in their bins or memes declared to be central by the individual during the narrative are given a more central location in the map.
7. Memes that share affective, connotative, or behavioral dimensions are linked in the map using edges.
8. Memes that are in conflict or in opposition with each other are shown as repelling each other.

With both methods, resultant memes are linked according to internal characteristics and displayed graphically. Typically, groups of memes form clusters with a common theme and the psychotherapist adds those identifying themes to the self-maps. The maps produced by either the "forty-persons" or "narrative" methods consist of cognitive pathways linking associated memes. The self also consists of non-rational and unconscious factors that trigger activation of various clusters of memes. These unconscious factors might include associations between emotional triggers and responses that appear to overrule rational cognitive responses. They can also include episodic reactions to mental conditions such as bipolar disorder that activate sequences of perception and behaviour embedded within separate clusters of the self. Unconscious facts can also be heritable. For example, after measuring for psychological characteristics including mental health, predisposing embedded emotions, and personality (e.g., "The Big Five" of extroversion, agreeableness, openness, conscientiousness, and neuroticism), the psychotherapist adds long range links to the self-map by which thematic clusters may be triggered. An inherited predisposition for introversion, for example, does not mean that the client will always exhibit the behaviours associated with introversion, but the behavioural sequences that signify introverted behaviour may be triggered, sometimes unpredictably. Mapping the mechanism by which introversion can trigger a known sequence of behaviors, allowing the client greater consciousness and control of the process.

The narrative method of self-map construction allows for more possible variations and less therapist or researcher influence on self-depiction and is, therefore, preferred from a research perspective. The more directive method requires less of the therapist's time. We have had good results in psychotherapy using both methods. Whichever method is used, it is crucial to actively involve the client in co-construction and interpretation. If the directive method is used, it is important to supplement the information gathering by soliciting the client's perspectives on structural dimensions and using information from taking the client's history to inform connections. For example, a failure to identify an emotive aspect to the self independent of affect attributed to individual memes should be explored to determine whether the client considers himself to be emotive or whether emotion is to be avoided. It is possible, using the "forty persons" method, that the failure to identify such an emotional base is a methodological oversight. Similarly, a failure to identify a volitional center using the directive method should not be interpreted as necessarily implying the client lacks volition; rather, the client's history and feelings with respect to self-empowerment should be explored further, leading to possible revisions. A comparison of the two methods of constructing memetic self-maps is shown in Table 1.

Table 1: A comparative outline of two methods of memetic self-map construction

	Self-Narrative Method	"Forty Persons" Method
1. Data Collection	The client or participant gives a detailed description of who they are. The researcher or therapist may give prompts to ensure a detailed description. The therapist asks about common self characteristics that may not be represented.	The client is asked to create four lists of who they are: ten persons that encompass roles, ten things they believe to be true, ten things they like about themselves, and ten things they would change about themselves if they could.
2. Manipulation of Data	The therapist transcribes the narrative and then codes each segment using the "constant comparative" method common to Grounded Theory (Glaser, 1992; Strauss, 1987) and Transcendental Realism (Kanis, 2004; Miles & Huberman, 1994)	The client is asked to rank order each item on each list from the easiest to hardest to give up. The therapist and client co-construct code names representing each item.
3. Identification of memes	The therapist places coded segments into "bins" for each code name. Those codings with connotative, behavioural, and affective characteristics are declared to be memes.	The therapist explores connotative, affective, and behavioural characteristics associated with each named item with the client. Those items that have all three characteristics are declared to be memes.
4. Arrangement of memes	Those memes representing a larger number of segments are placed centrally. Those with similar connotation, affect, or implied behaviours are viewed as connected. If one meme leads to another behaviourally then those memes are also linked.	Memes that have been prioritized as more important by the client are placed more centrally on their self-map. Memes sharing the same characteristics (connotative, affective, or behavioural) are considered linked. Those that lead behaviourally to other memes are considered linked.

5. Identification of clusters	Groups of memes that may act in concert when triggered (as in a script) or may present as a "mini-self" in particular contexts are identified.	Groups of memes that may act in concert when triggered (as in a script) or may present as a "mini-self" in particular contexts are identified.
6. Non-memetic factors	The therapist and client explore personality characteristics, traumas, illnesses, and other predispositions that may trigger meme clusters. These are placed at the bottom of the self-map.	The therapist and client explore personality characteristics, traumas, illnesses, and other predispositions that may trigger meme clusters. These are placed at the bottom of the self-map.

Both methods of identifying memes (the 40 persons and the narrative approaches) have been used to create self-maps that have been effective in psychotherapy. The "40 persons" method may be described as "top down" in that potential memes are identified but subsequent interviewing is required to detail the full and rich descriptions necessary to define the meme in question and its context and application. With the narrative approach, the full and rich description of the self is the starting point, with memes emerging from the data through subsequent analysis. Exemplars of both methods are examined in this manual. Self-mapping, by either approach, appears to be compatible with a variety of therapeutic approaches.

3

An Initial Cognitive Self-map

The "Forty-Persons" Method

This is a detailed re-examination of the case study that served as the introduction to *The Evolved Self* (Robertson, 2020). It traces the development and use of self-mapping in the treatment of a youth identified in the literature as "Suzie." Memes were identified using the "Forty Persons" method and a map of the youth's self was prepared by connecting related memes. A successful treatment plan followed the mapping exercise. This account outlines the steps taken to achieve this success.

Ethical considerations preclude the use of control groups for life-threatening conditions (Hvid & Wang, 2009; Karver et al., 2008), thus novel approaches often flow from innovations made in the direct counselling experience. The technique of memetic self-mapping began as such an innovation. It began after the failure of more traditional approaches to reduce the suicide ideation experienced by Suzie.

She had attempted suicide on five occasions before she was eighteen. In making a referral to one of the authors (LHR), Suzie's initial therapist stated that she had been compliant with treatment but remained "high-risk" after twenty months of treatment that included cognitive behavioural therapy (CBT) and antidepressant medication. As part of a new risk assessment, Suzie presented with an elevated risk of re-attempting on *The Suicide Probability Scale* (Cull & Gill, 1988) with clinically significant subscale scores (above the 98th percentile) for low self-esteem, anger, suicide ideation, and depression. A published case study (Robertson, 2011) described several childhood traumatic events and a dysfunctional family dynamic that contributed to her suicide ideation. Since CBT has proven efficacy (Dozois, 2002; Warwar & Greenberg, 2000) and since the nature of the therapeutic relationship affects outcomes (Hyer et al., 2004; Ryum & Stiles, 2005), it was decided to continue with CBT. An attempt was made to normalize some experiences and reframe others so as to empower the client to see herself as a competent actor and problem solver. The therapist and client co-developed behavioural "homework" assignments that included positive affirmations, meaningful and enjoyable activity, regular physical activity, and reality testing to discover the accuracy (or inaccuracy) of perceived slights from teachers and others. Suzie was initially compliant and enthusiastically so, but after initial improvement, her suicide ideation and rumination returned. We attempted to deal with family of origin issues using techniques from Adlerian psychotherapy and childhood trauma using Eye Movement Desensitization and Reprocessing (EMDR). Each technique resulted in short-term relief of symptoms followed by relapse. Finally, with an affected air of professional assurance, the therapist suggested the creation of a map of her self to identify what was blocking treatment.

Identifying and Placing Memes in Suzie's Self

An implication of defining each meme as a complex of connotative, affective, and behavioral factors is that each cultural unit is individualized. For example, it is not likely that any two people will understand the meme for marriage in exactly the same way, although they may agree on the underlying concept. Thus, Suzie needed to identify her memes using referent words available to her but linkages between memes would depend on the individualized qualities of each.

We began by identifying referent words Suzie used to describe herself, and then we explored the qualities of each referent. She was asked to list ten "persons" or roles that represented her. For example, she was a daughter, but whether that factual statement represented a way that she chose to define herself on a list of ten was another matter. In fact, "daughter" did not appear on her list of ten persons that included, in rank order: father hater, depressed person, writer, feminist, dancer, dramatic person, sister hater, singer, friend, and collector of heart-shaped boxes.

The list was rank-ordered using a sorting exercise. Each of her ten persons was placed on index cards, and she was asked which of these persons or roles would be the easiest to give up, second easiest, and so on. On this exercise, "father hater" was the meme she would have the most difficulty giving up while "heart-shaped boxes" would be the easiest. This was interpreted to mean that at this point in her life, "father hater" was most central to her self-definition, "depressed person" was second most central, and "writer" third.

Suzie was then asked to create three additional self-defining lists in similar fashion: ten things I like about myself, ten things I would change about myself if I could, and ten things I believe to be true. Each meme was explored to ensure it contained connotative, affective, and behavioural dimensions. Referent words or phrases were selected on the basis of how the meme defined her in some way. The memes were then rank-ordered with those memes judged by her to be the most difficult to give up deemed to be more central to her being.

Items from all four lists were coded, and items judged to be reflections of the same meme were combined. For example, the client identified herself as a feminist (#4 on the "Ten Persons" exercise), and she said that one of the things she believed to be true was that women needed to fight for equality. Following further discussion to ensure the client's understanding was correctly interpreted; this belief was taken to reflect her understanding of feminism.

Items displaying referent, connotative, affective, and behavioural properties were deemed to be memes. For example, Suzie identified herself as a collector of heart-shaped boxes. These boxes were associated with romantic love, which was considered to be desirable but beyond her reach. She experienced wistfulness coupled with feelings of emptiness and loss associated with these boxes, which she collected and displayed. Table 2 lists these referent, connotative, emotive, and behavioural dimensions.

Table 2: **Dimensions of the meme "heart-shaped boxes" in the self of Suzie**

Dimension	Description
Referent	Frequently associated with Valentine's Day that are often used to carry chocolates
Connotation	Associated with romantic love, something desirable but probably beyond the reach of the youth
Affect	Wistfulness coupled with feelings of emptiness and loss
Associated behaviour	Collecting empty heart-shaped boxes of various sizes

The meme labelled "heart-shaped boxes" represented on the youth's self-map (Figure 4) is taken to include these connotative, affective, and behavioural dimensions. Since the boxes connoted romantic love, a line representing attractive force was drawn between it and a meme for love. The client's behaviour associated with these boxes was considered to be a dramatic expression of her associated emotions, so this meme was linked to another labelled "dramatic person." Being a collector of heart-shaped boxes was given the rank of ten in the "Ten Persons" exercise, so it was placed on the periphery of her self-map.

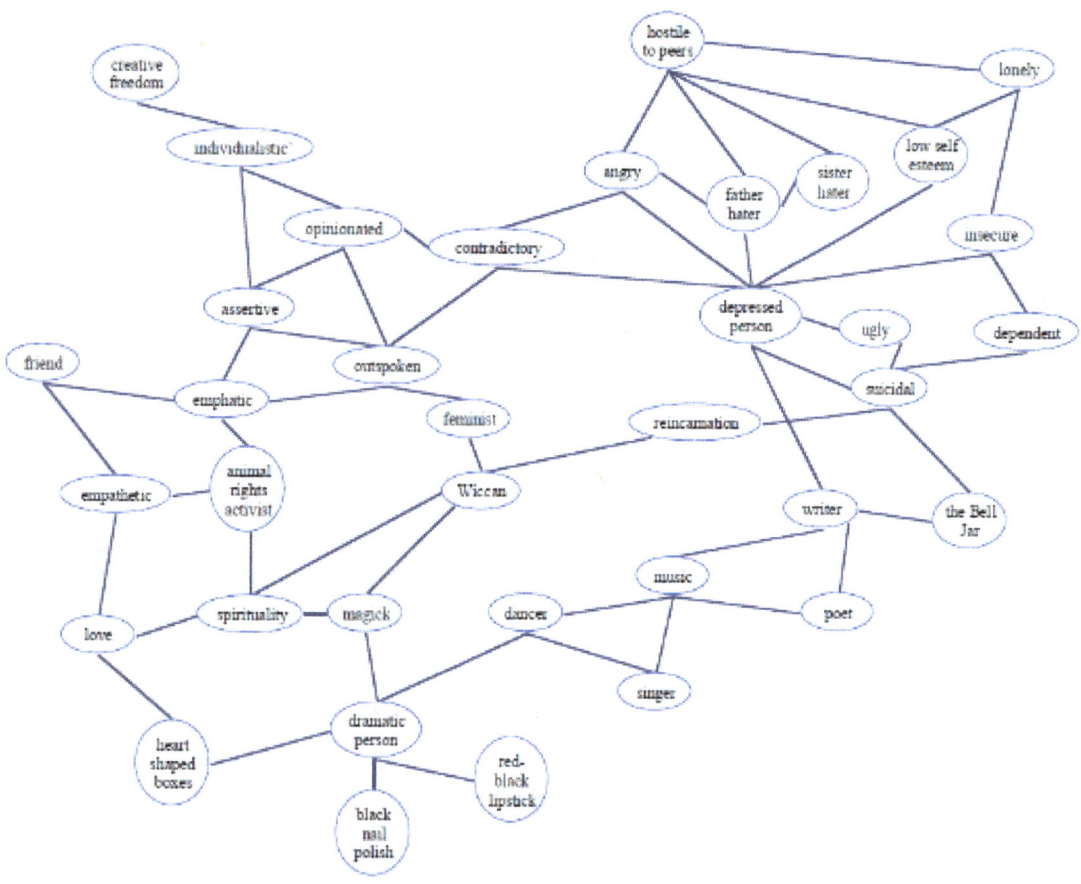

Figure 4: Initial self-map of Suzie with edges between memes representing shared connotative, affective or behavioural dimensions

The memes the client would have the most difficulty giving up were deemed to be more core or central to her identity and were placed in a more central position. Memes that shared connotative, affective, or behavioural properties were considered linked. Since linkages were viewed as analogous to forces of attraction, the positioning of individual memes shifted to represent those forces. The self-map in Figure 4 was a co-construction resulting from negotiation and revision with the client having the final say on where items fit on her map.

Eight edges or links lead from "depressed person" to other memes in Suzie's self. In retrospect, it should not have been too surprising that this meme appeared as the hub or core of her self-definition. Dozois & Dobson (2001) found that depressed individuals have an interconnected negative self-representational system and lack a well-organized positive template of self. The qualitative difference between having "depressed person" as part of one's self and merely being depressed was explored in De Man & Gutierrez's (2002) study into the stability of self-esteem. After factoring out the effects of depression, they found that unstable self-esteem correlated with suicide ideation in those with low self-esteem but not with those with high self-esteem scores, concluding, "For those with low self-esteem, stable self-esteem may serve a protective function, whereas instability of self-esteem may be a good predictor of suicidal thinking" (p. 237). This accords with findings that the initial lifting of depression in youth, especially through the use of antidepressant medication, may increase suicidal behaviour (Fritz, 2007). If instability of self results in increased suicide risk among those with low self-esteem and depression, then Suzie's subconscious resistance to therapy while actively complying with treatment can be seen as a self-protective measure.

Not only did Suzie's "depressed person" meme obtain scores indicating centrality (#2 on the "ten persons" exercise), but it was connected to more memes (8) than any other. Those eight memes, "ugly," "suicidal," "father hater," "contradictory," "low self-esteem," "angry," "insecure," and "writer," were all defined in self-defeating ways. For example, the client felt herself to be a bad person for hating her father. She defined herself as having "low self-esteem," and believed this was a permanent state of being. Her writing included gory images of pain and death with an underlying theme of self-denunciation.

Some memes not directly connected to "depressed person" were viewed to be part of a cluster supporting suicidal behaviour. Her belief in reincarnation supported suicide ideation with the connotation that she could not "come back" in a worse condition than she presently experienced. Self-defining memes labeled "dependent," "lonely," and "hostile to peers" also supported her pattern of suicide ideation.

An objective of therapy was to relieve the client's depression, but imagine the self illustrated in Figure 4 without the "depressed person" meme. We can see that the whole structure would become less stable with two general clusters, one including her family and the other including her activities outside of her family, connected by just two gateway memes: anger and suicidal. From this we can see that Suzie's instinctive and unconscious resistance to even antidepressant medication may have saved her life, but the structure led to increased depressive rumination. Figure 5 illustrates her most common ruminative cycle.

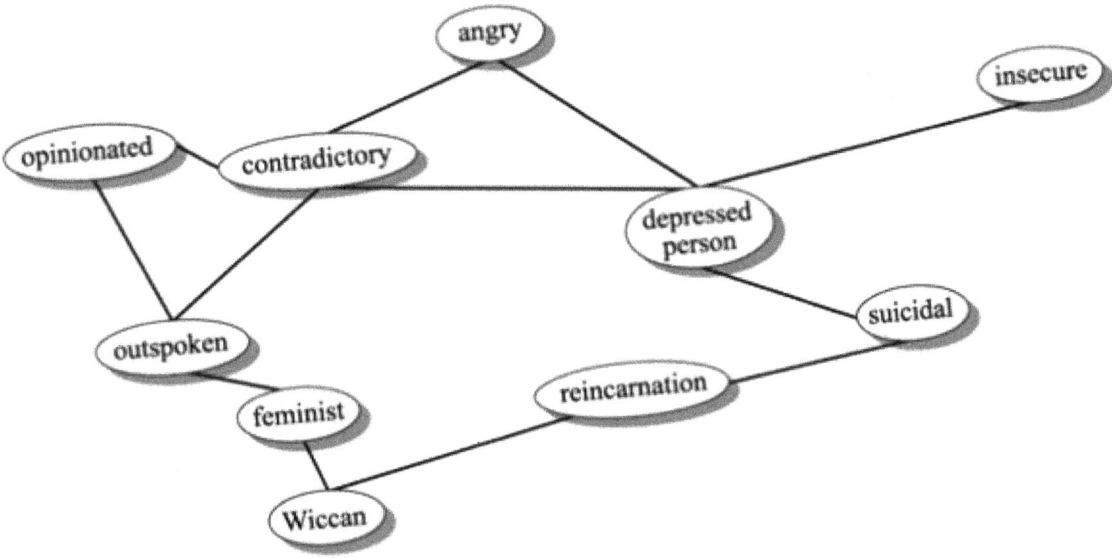

Figure 5: An illustration of memetic ruminative paths or routes leading to suicide ideation in the self of "Suzie"

Each meme in a self-map has associations with adjoining memes that may be taken as the outline of a story. A ruminative pattern occurs when thoughts are directed in a cyclical pattern with few opportunities to "get off the cycle" by engaging in other thoughts. Concomitantly, since there is no beginning, the cycle allows many entry points. For example, external or internal events or associations may trigger the client to recall her self-identifier as "outspoken." This, in turn, leads to the association of being contradictory (or contradicted) with an associated emotion of anger. But Suzie's "angry" meme included an element of impotence - her anger, whether expressed or internalized, rarely led to a positive outcome. This habitually fed her depression, which, in turn, led to thoughts that she may as well be (or would be better off being) dead. Present in Figure 4 but not illustrated in Figure 5 is a short cycle involving thinking about reincarnation, leading to "The Bell Jar" (a book about a suicidal youth), dependency or being ugly - all of which eventually led back to depression. Figure 5 illustrates a longer cycle where thoughts about how her life would be better after reincarnation would lead to the Wiccan religion with which she identified. She liked the non-patriarchal nature of Wicca and this led to thoughts of feminism, which returned her to being outspoken. The memes are non-directional, with the result the self-story could also proceed from "outspoken" to "feminist," "Wiccan," "reincarnation," "suicidal," and "depression."

While a map can never be the complete terrain, examining the initial representation in figure 4 allowed insight into why traditional psychotherapeutic methods had been insufficient in this case. "Depressed person" was so central to her self-map that it became clear other more peripheral memes would need to be removed or relocated before success could be achieved. We would need to construct a new, alternate core meme within a revised self before the depressive meme could be removed entirely. Some memes could be reframed, which in memetic terminology involves changing emotive or connotative aspects. The distinction between assessment and therapy is rarely discrete. The therapist had already been engaged in a process of reframing when Suzie and the therapist co-constructed her map.

Reconstructing the Self: Reframing and Modifying Memes

Suzie had attacked people, verbally and physically, who had mistreated cats or dogs, and had established a reputation as an angry person, and the therapist had suggested a label that connoted a reframe: "animal rights activist." The reframe required that she focus on an element already present in the meme—that she had a concern for the well-being of these animals. She had also challenged teachers and other adults for infringing on the rights of children and youth. The label "outspoken" was chosen to encompass times when she confronted others. She believed that women and girls suffered from sexism, and she embraced feminism. She believed that the Christianity of her parents was oppressive and embraced a spirituality that emphasized feminist values. This emphasis on rights met the Adlerian definition of "social interest"—the" impulse to improve or protect the community in some ways. While this may be understood as an essential ingredient of a healthy, functioning self (Adler, 1929; Dryden et al., 2001; Robertson, 2010), Suzie's social interest was, at this point, an interpretation of actions committed in anger. The therapist began to consider that these diffuse often angry responses could interpretively support a healthy new core to her self that would rival "depressed person" for centrality.

Visualizing herself in map form coincided with Suzie's determination to override the defensive or protective measures described in the previous subsection and engage in a process of self-change. The map gave her a sense of the totality that made her and that she would remain a unique entity with continuity while in the midst of change. Thus, the self-map, as opposed to the core meme within the map that we were seeking to change, served to preserve a sense of her continuity. The therapist suggested the presence of a new core meme, 'human rights," that united her feminism, children's and animal rights with the reported "feel" that it had always been there, unrecognized. The new location of this new human rights meme is pictured in Figure 6.

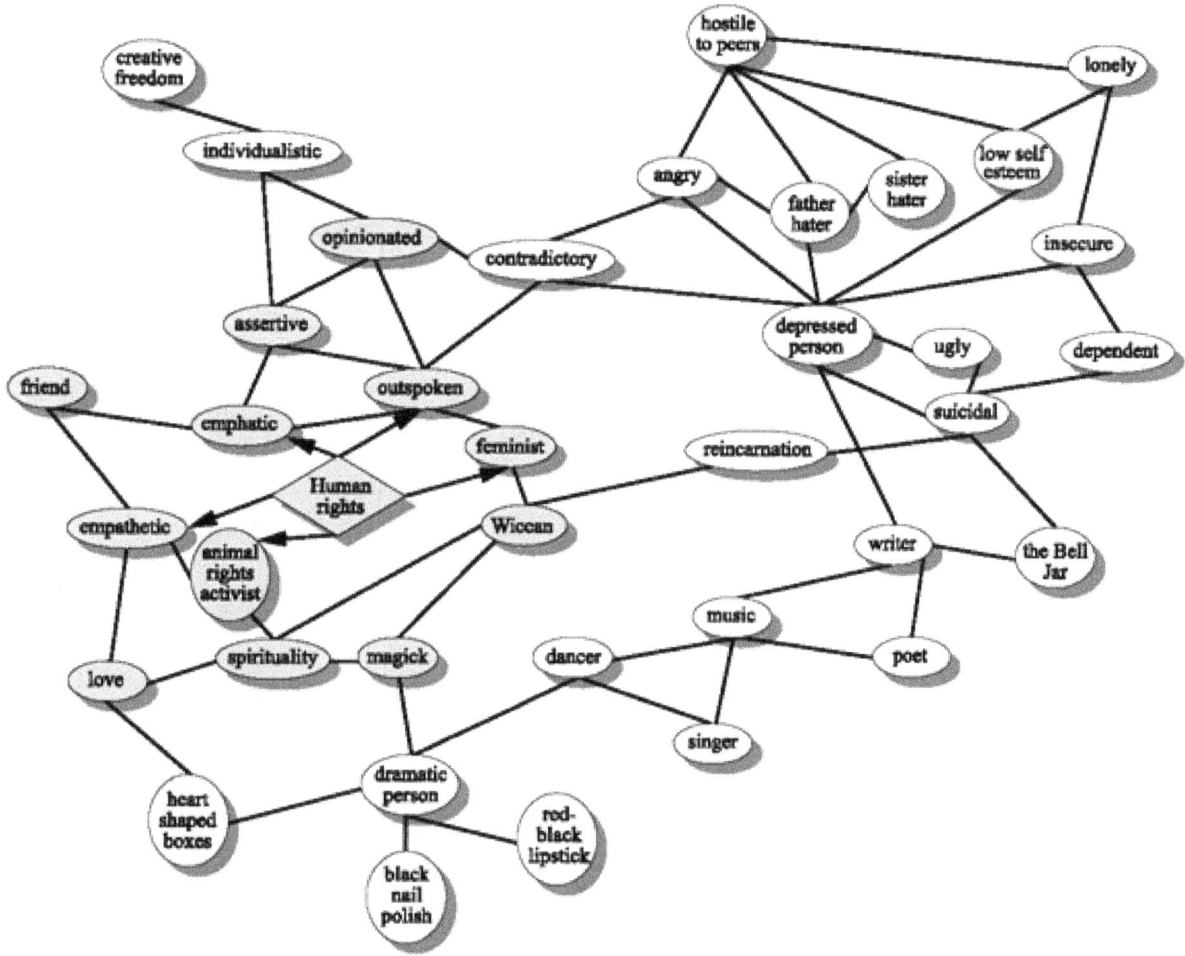

Figure 6: A revised memetic self. A suicidal youth showing the location of a co-constructed new core meme – "human rights" with supporting memes highlighted

Suzie was able to visualize the scripts she followed in her depressive cycle. Since memes are connected by emotive, connotative, and behavioural forces represented by vectors, she was able to trace how her thoughts tended to follow routes traced by those vectors as though she had ben following a script. Awareness of these thought patterns allowed Suzie to change the direction of her thoughts at predetermined nodes (represented by memes) in the cycle.

Situating "depressed person" within a cluster of related memes allowed for the co-construction of a treatment plan aimed at shifting it to a more peripheral location while still maintaining Suzie's sense of continuity with her past. Although she had previously defined herself as a writer, Suzie had written from her depression, thus reinforcing the dysfunctional core meme with that label; however, she now began to write from her new "human rights" center. The cognitive and behavioural plan developed to shift Suzie's writer self from supporting her depression to supporting her "human rights" meme also served to strengthen two structural components common to healthy functioning selves—community and volition.

In similar evolutionary fashion, Suzie was encouraged to redirect her anger externally in ways that would promote social interest. The energy provided by her anger was now directed toward her outspokenness and associated social causes with the immediate benefit of channeling self-defeating impotent anger to a growing sense of self-empowerment. Other memes, peripheral to but supportive of her depression, were eliminated entirely. For example, she saw herself as ugly, but "ugly" was not supported by a large cluster of memes, so it was possible to have her perform "homework" assignments designed to challenge that belief. She discovered that most of her peers viewed her to be attractive.

The mapping activity allowed us to see which memes had less support and would be more easily removed from Suzie's self. Once removed, those memes no longer lent support to more ingrained dysfunctional aspects of the self, and we were able to shift some memes (e.g., writer, poet, music) to support functional core memes by using behavioural "homework" assignments. After seven months of this therapy, Suzie's map (figure 7) illustrated a self that was far more functional.

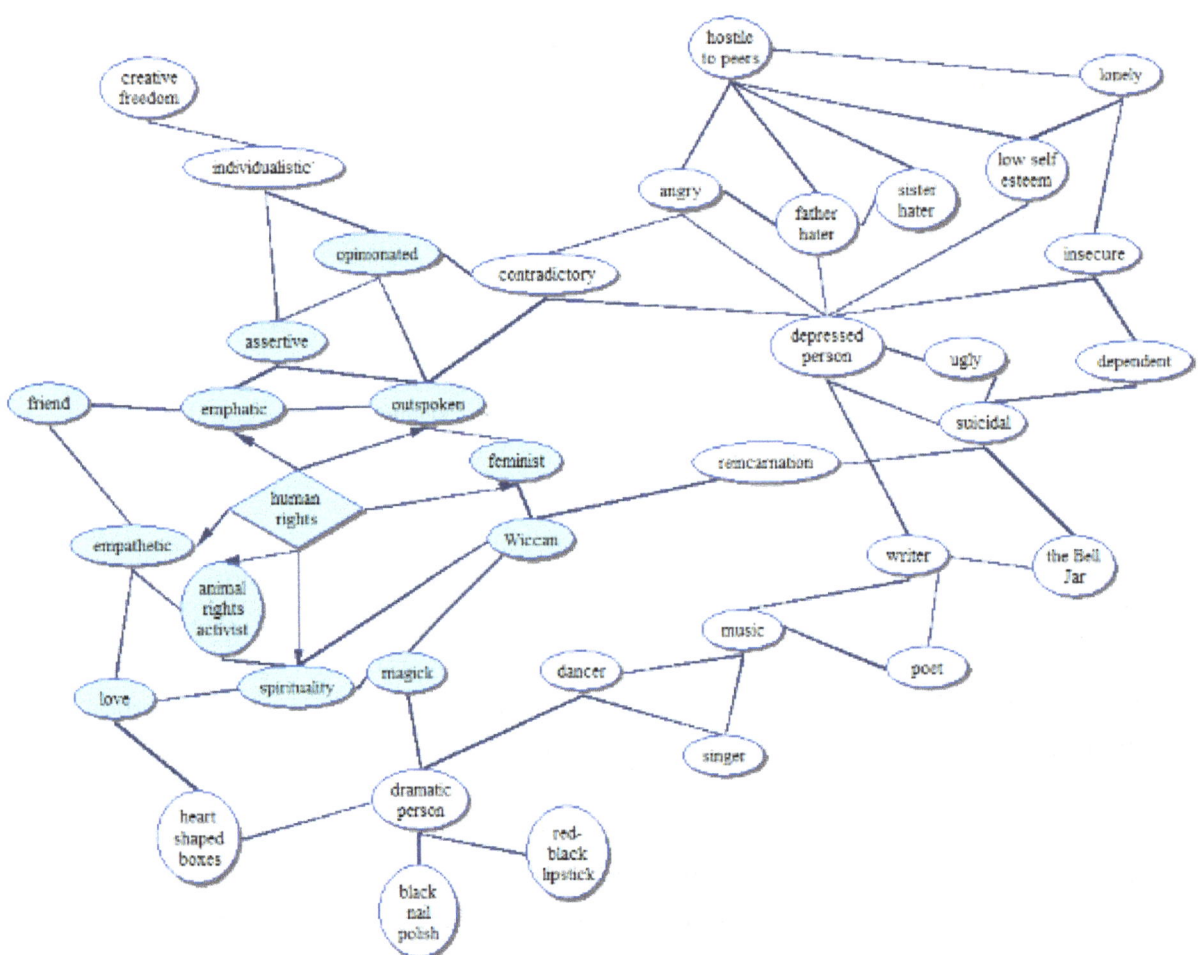

Figure 7: Self-map illustrating changes in self-definition resulting from "homework assignments" designed to support the new core meme "human rights"

With "depressed person" receiving less support from surrounding memes in Suzie's self, it became possible to re-frame it, not as a self-defining meme, but as one emotion among many. If we were to view the self as purely a cognitive structure, then at this point we eliminated depression from the suicidal youth's self. A more nuanced view is that depression is an emotion that we may experience without the necessity of defining ourselves by it.

What schools of psychotherapy could utilize self-mapping?

A case study of the mapping technique used in therapy with Suzie (Chapter 3) was presented to a graduate class in counselling psychology at the University of Calgary. A cognitive behaviourist noted that Suzie was prompted to challenge some ineffective and obsessive cognitions using visual stimulation provided by a cognitive map, and she re-enforced a more useful set of self-cognitions using behavioural "homework" assignments. He suggested that what was being used here was CBT. "Not so," declared a narrative therapist who ventured that the youth changed her personal story to see herself as an activating agent capable of dealing with unfortunate circumstances in her life. In this interpretation, the self-map provided Suzie with an outline to understand how she had structured her previous self-narrative so she might change it. The training received by the first author (LHR) in Adlerian psychotherapy pictured the self as core to a more encompassing "worldview." This Adlerian concept is similar to CBT's "cognitive schema" or narrative therapy's "constructed reality" and memetic self-mapping fits comfortably with all three; and indeed, is compatible with all psychotherapies that define the human mind as capable of self-reflection.

Cognitive-behavioural methods used to combat depression often emphasize hedonic pleasure, as when clients are encouraged to list and engage in activities that were perceived to have been enjoyable in the past, but life satisfaction and meaning may be related to meaning-making separate from positive and negative affect. The development of a new human rights meme to replace Suzie's "depressed person" core was an example of such meaning-making. If happiness is related to believing in something bigger than oneself, then linking transcendent purpose to a client's volitional ability will reduce depression. But "depressed person" was part of Suzie's self, so concomitant with building eudamonic purpose, we needed to remove or reduce support for the "depressed person" meme. Eudaimonic purpose references the satisfaction of self-fulfillment irrespective of personal circumstance that can be restrictive and quite painful.

The suicidal client shifted from feelings of impotent anger and sadness to action based on her core beliefs and values. The visualization afforded by self-mapping assisted her in reflectively developing an orientation to challenge the cognitive schemata that kept her in a self-destructive cycle. From the Adlerian perspective, the map-making exercise would be understood as a way of empowering the client to make changes to her worldview by coupling a psycho-educational approach with an appeal to social interest.

From the perspective of narrative therapy, the youth changed her personal story to one where she was an activating agent capable of dealing with unfortunate life circumstances. With this interpretation, the self-map was an outline helping the client to understand how she had structured her previous self-narrative, giving her the opportunity to change the plot, and she was able to replace that plot of ineffective victimhood with a personal outline suggestive of agency or volition.

The construction of the self-map in this case study allowed both the client and her therapist to visualize the client's self, agree on goals for change, and plan incremental changes leading to the realization of those goals. That the process of self-map construction and treatment is consistent with a range of theoretical approaches is not surprising if we recall that the idea of the mind as something that stands apart from the physical world so as to observe it and is capable of internally consistent thought is central to the practice of psychology.

4

Creating a Self-Map using the Narrative Approach

We are storytellers. When invited to describe who they are, people will very often use their episodic memory to tell a remembered story, or a series of stories, illustrating their qualities or describe how they would react in different situations. Recalled anecdotes add illustration, context, and flavour to personal characteristics, dispositions, and traits. Open-ended conversation permits a full exploration of themes, but not without drawbacks. We are predisposed to selection bias (Bhogal, 2023; Pinker, 2021), and the stories we tell about ourselves often tend to cast us in a good or sympathetic light. Further, the stories we tell will be influenced or primed by preceding events. The clinician using the narrative method to create self-maps will need to be alert to such gaps and use supplemental questions to ensure full and rich descriptions using open-ended questions such as those listed in Chapter 2.

Once we are satisfied that we have a full and rich description of the person, then we need to begin identifying memes from the transcript. Modeled on a method developed by Miles and Huberman (1994), we recommend segmenting transcribed interviews into units of thought with each unit coded for substance or main idea that is illustrated in what can be called "descriptive coding." All of the segments with the same descriptive code are grouped together in a "bin." The contents of each bin are examined to determine if, collectively, these segments satisfy the definition of "meme." Do they collectively exhibit connotative, affective, and behavioural characteristics that provide the forces of attraction that animate memes (the referent component is already present as the descriptive code)? Those codes that do not fit the definition of a meme are either discarded entirely or included as properties of the memes that have already been identified as such. It is possible for one segment to be coded for more than one meme. Memes appearing in the same segment were considered connected unless the participant was contrasting those memes. Memes that referred to other memes explicitly or implicitly in their referent, connotative, affective, or behavioral dimensions were also considered connected. Through this process a map forms consisting of a finite number of memes that were differentially connected to each other. Such maps are prepared by the researcher to be returned to the client in a subsequent interview.

In hermeneutic fashion, data collection and analysis proceed in a cyclical fashion with more data collected and maps amended until the map resonates cognitively and emotionally with the client; that is, the client identifies with the map at a feeling level. Participants are invited to discuss ways that their map could be strengthened, and they are invited to elaborate on issues that came to mind while viewing their maps. Sometimes, resonance is achieved with the first iteration, but from our experience, two sessions are likely. Occasionally, three cycles result in the client identifying with the self-map. It is important to note that these narrative sessions are often about 2 hours long.

Once resonance is achieved, clients are invited to reflect on things that happened in their past that helped make their present selves. They are invited to share any new thoughts or feelings about who they are as a result of developing this map of themselves. Invite them to look for relationships between memes or clusters of memes (thematic coding). Ask clients if there had been any changes that had occurred since the first interview and whether looking at their map led them to think of changes that they would want to make to their selves. In point form, the narrative method of self-mapping can be summarized thus:

1. Using an open-ended, semi-structured interview format, record the client's self-narratives;
2. The clinician or researcher transcribes the interview;
3. The interview is segmented and descriptive codes are used to label each segment;
4. The segments with the same descriptive code are placed in a "bin," and each bin is then examined collectively for four memetic dimensions - referent, connotation, affect, and behaviour.
5. Memes with more segments in their "bin," are thought to be more central in the individual's self; memes that share connotative, affective or behavioural characteristics are considered linked;
6. Memes identified in this manner are placed in map form;
7. Themes (interpretive codes) are noted as they appeared to relate to relationships among memes;
8. These graphic displays are presented to clients during subsequent interviews for the purpose of confirming, elaborating, and correcting.

Using the Narrative Approach: An Example

She was initially reticent. When asked to tell me about herself, "Tina" said she was in her twenties, had three children, was married, and liked to clean[1]. When prompted further, she explained that talking about herself was difficult, but her responses gradually lengthened, producing 15 pages of transcript. A transcript of Tina's initial interview was divided into 52 segments and each segment was given at least one code word identifying a key aspect of the segment. The segments coded with the same words were then grouped together in the same "bin," and emergent characteristics were examined in comparison with the structure used in defining meme, and words satisfying that definition were retained as memes. The "bin" for mother used in constructing Tina's self, showing how text was segmented and coded, is reproduced in Appendix "A."

More segments were coded for "mother" (eleven) than any other meme, reflecting the importance Tina placed on being a mother to her self-definition. That meme was set in relation to Tina's other identified memes in her initial self-map reproduced in figure 8. The full list of memes used in constructing this self-map showing referent, connotative, affective, and behavioural dimensions of each meme is presented in Appendix "B."

Tina believed that being a good mother involved ensuring that her four children had many opportunities to play. In one segment describing her role as mother, she said:

> I take the kids out if they're nice. I don't spoil them to the fact that I give them whatever they want, but they do have a lot of stuff that a lot of kids don't have, like games and systems like they probably have every game system available, except for PlayStation. They got 2 Xboxes, 1 Xbox 360, a computer in their room - they just have lots of stuff, lots and lots of stuff.

In another segment, coded for "mother," Tina revealed that she saw her children's behaviour as a reflection on her as a parent, followed by a second segment, in the same paragraph, that indicated that mothering also implied a concern for children's safety:

> I get compliments, people telling me, "Oh, you've got such really good kids, well mannered," and they never say, "What?" they always say, "Pardon me, please and thank you," we're really hard on them, really strict. We don't let them do much, not as much as, like they wanna go play in the bush. They can't do that. I used to be able to when I was a kid, but I won't let my kids go in there. They always have to be around me to make sure I know they're safe, and, yeah, I'm very proud of the way they turned out."

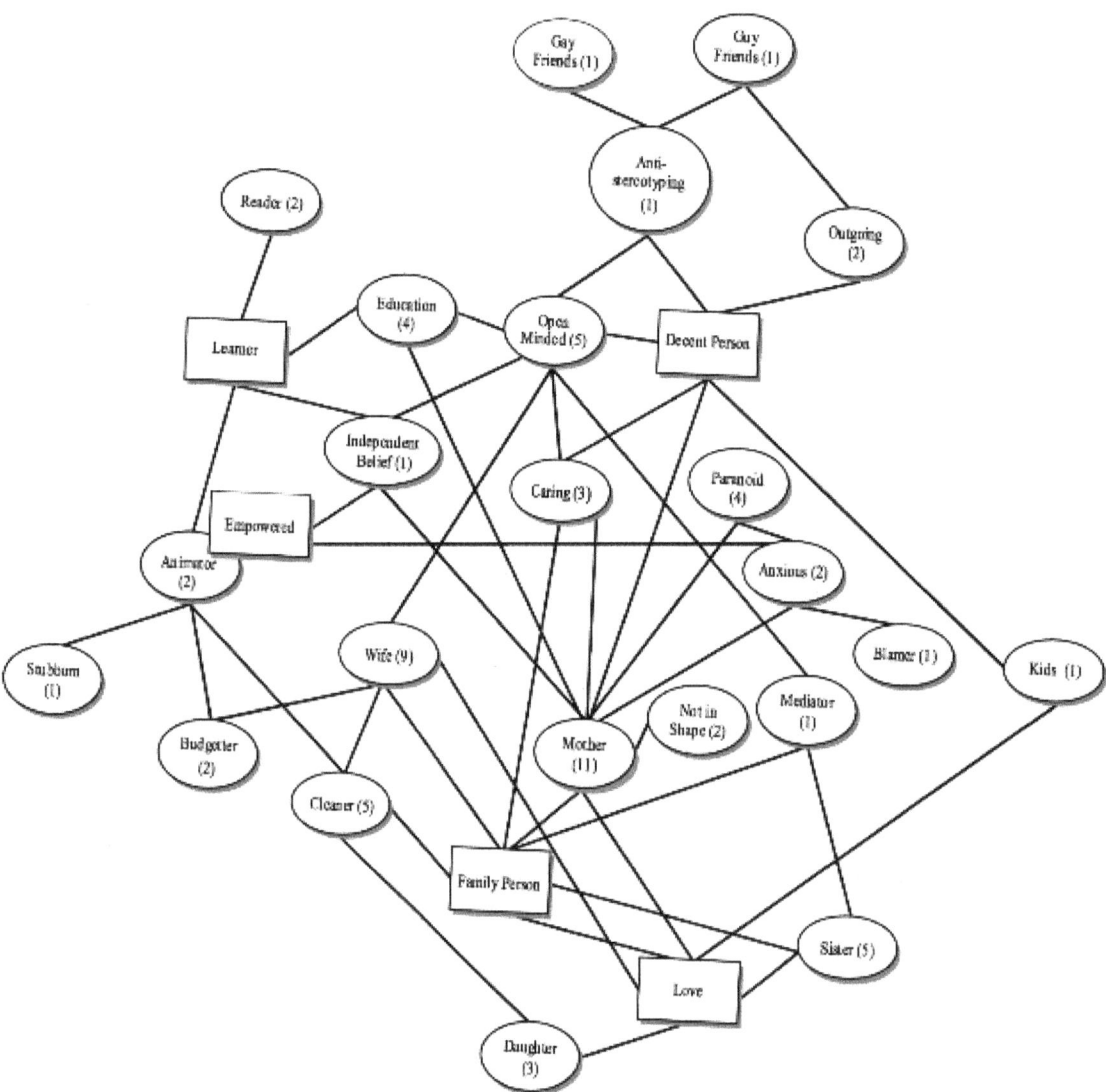

Figure 8: Memetic map of Tina resulting from the segmentation and coding of her initial interview showing the number segments coded for each meme (in brackets)

Tina was still an adolescent when she lost her firstborn to "crib death," an event that followed the death of a half-sister, whom she had met two years previously. Tina linked these two events to explain her anxiety disorder, which she referred to as her paranoia. She viewed "paranoid" as a self-defining meme linked with "mother" in the following segment:

> I only got to know my son for 6 months, 25 days and I only knew my sister for 2 years, so yeah, you take every moment in. I think that's why I'm so paranoid with him (her newest baby) as well, he won't sleep by himself, I have a baby heart monitor, breath monitor, I just won't leave him alone.

Since the above segment was coded for both "mother" and "paranoid," a link was drawn between the two in figure 8. We can see from this, and the following segment, being a responsible mother connoted paranoia with a resultant set of behaviours.

> There's nothing gonna happen to him, nothing at all. The only thing I don't have is a video camera monitor, and actually that's something I'm thinking about getting too, so he can sleep in the room by himself without me freaking out going in there every five minutes so.

While explicitly referencing her sister and father, the following short segment also showed independence of action from the opinion of her father. The segment was coded for "independent belief," "mother," and "sister," with the existence of all three memes in one paragraph indicating linkages between each. The process of individuation from her father, who had a different response to these deaths, is an indicator that Tina had developed a sense of her own uniqueness and volition.

> I have pictures of (the son that died of crib death) and I have pictures of (the sister who died two years after she met her) all over the house, and I don't think he (her father) likes that, but I don't care; I don't take them down.

Several segments suggested the importance of ensuring her children excelled in school as part of mothering. Other segments connected Tina's meme "mother" with not being in shape, being anxious, caring, and the themes "Love," "Family Person," and "Decent Person."

Love was a recurrent theme in Tina's self-narrative. The following segment could have been coded for "daughter," "mother," "sister," "wife," "brother," "husband," and "kids," but instead it was declared to be a theme within her self that she applies to both present and future relationships. It is displayed in Figure 8 in a rectangle as opposed to the usual oval and it is positioned as central to a cluster of memes that include relationships in which she displays this love. This emotion forms a theme that infuses her relationships:

> Love for my kids, the way I feel about my mom and dad, sister, brother, husband my kids, and uh, the way I love them and take care of them, pamper them, make sure they're ok, I don't think that will ever change about myself, I'll always have that, that bond with them, and I don't think that will ever change.

Love was an emotion Tina associated with being a mother, daughter, and sister and was also given to other children not her own. Had she described herself as a "lover," then that might have qualified as a meme in its own right, but she did not. On the other hand, "love" is very much a theme in her life. Other thematic centres represented in Figure 8 include "family person," "Decent Person," "Empowered," and "Learner." As can be seen from the example of Tina's meme "mother," each meme represents a large amount of individualized information, and this information can be summarized under the headings Referent, Connotation, Affect, and Behaviour. This information is listed using the four components of the meme in Table 3.

Table 3: The Memetic Properties of Tina's meme "mother"

Referent	A biological fact associated with bearing children
Connotation	Maternal responsibility to those children to shape their behaviour and ensure their future success.
Affect	Love, caring, valuing of children
Behaviour	Ensures that her children are safe, cared for, read to, go to school and do

For Tina at the time of her initial self-map illustrated in Figure 8, being a mother is to be anxious about her children's well-being. "Anxious" was, therefore, connected to "mother" and was pictured as a separate but closely related meme from "paranoid." Her "anxious" and "paranoid" memes are summarized in Table 4.

Table 4: A Comparison of Tina's Linked Memes for "Anxious" and "Paranoid"

	Anxious	Paranoid
Referent	Suffers from anxiety/panic attacks (1-2 times per month)	Excessive concern over the safety of her children

Connotation	There is something wrong with her mental health	Mothers are responsible when bad things happen to their children
Affect	Distress	Worry
Behaviour	Goes away from others and talks herself out of bouts of panic/anxiety	Monitors children continually; won't allow them to play in the bush behind their house

Tina's anxiety was also associated with motherhood. It is possible that the referent words "paranoid" and "anxiety" represented the same meme, but the decision to code the two as separate was subjectively based on the understanding that she had previously been diagnosed as having an anxiety disorder and part of her self-definition was someone who suffers from this condition. At the time of this study, she was no longer taking medication or counselling. When she recognized panic symptoms, she would go into a separate room and talk or will herself out of it, leading to a sense of empowerment. The second most referenced meme with nine segments illustrated in Figure 8 is "wife," and connections were formed between it and memes for budgeters, cleaners, and open-minded people. The central memes to Tina's being was that of being a mother and a wife, with both connected to "Caring." "Caring" would be a descriptive attribute for many people without being a meme; but for Tina, "Caring" had the four elements of the meme and formed part of her self-definition as a caring person. "Caring" is illustrated in Table 5.

Table 5: Tina's meme "Caring" showing referent, connotative, affective, and behavioural aspects

Referent	A feeling that suggests the well-being of others is important to one's self
Connotation	Decent people care about others.
Affect	A feeling of closeness and responsibility for others

Behaviour	Cares for her parents by taking care of their needs, defend people who are stigmatized, worries about her children and others. Attaches the concept of decency to the act of caring.

Although "open-minded" can also be an adjective, for Tina "open-minded" was set as a meme that was used to define herself as a good and worthwhile person. She used the act of accepting people of different cultural and religious beliefs, orientations, and practices as the referent for this meme. She believed that people who exhibit this quality are "decent" and share the perception that all people are good. The quality of easy-going acceptance was associated with this meme, although she admitted that she did not always exhibit this affect. She strived to welcome people of different religious perspectives, sexual orientations, and cultures into her home. In attempting to be open-minded, Tina also accepted that her husband may have additional (but approved) sexual liaisons with other women with the limitation that if he ever lied about it, it would "break my heart."

As we began to illustrate in discussing Tina, the self is a complexity containing a huge amount of information that cannot be held in the mind of the client or counsellor in its entirety. Self-mapping is a way of reducing the complexity by summarizing and labeling units of that complexity. By setting memes that in themselves represent larger quantities of information in relation to each other, we can see the self holistically. But like any map, it is a simplification; it is not the actual terrain.

Recognizing Complexity in Building upon the Basic Self-Map

The data used to create the self-map in figure 8 was obtained from one two-hour interview. The process of segmenting, coding, and creating the map took another five clinician hours using a qualitative research software package. The map reproduced in Figure 8 was subsequently presented to Tina in a second two-hour interview. At this time she was invited to discuss ways the map could more accurately represent herself.

Tina had previously been prescribed medication for depression and anxiety, but she refused to take this medication because she wanted to feel all her emotions. She admitted that she could not take her children to a mall because of social anxiety, yet she said she does not like the way she feels on medication because she "should be feeling everything." With further questioning she said, "Because that is part of life. To feel is part of life.... That's who I am." She added that a repertoire of emotions such as "sad, happy, mad, confused, and distant" is necessary to feel human. The repertoire of accessible human emotions is represented by a bar at the bottom of Tina's self-map in figure 9 with thick arrows flowing to and through various memes that are frequently triggered, or in turn trigger, these emotions.

In a moment of insight, Tina said bouts of depression and guilt prevented other emotions from surfacing; that is, when she felt guilt or depression, she was unable to feel her other emotions. As a result, a small bar was added to her self self-map, illustrated in Figure 9, representing how depression and guilt served to block other feelings emanating from her menu of emotions.

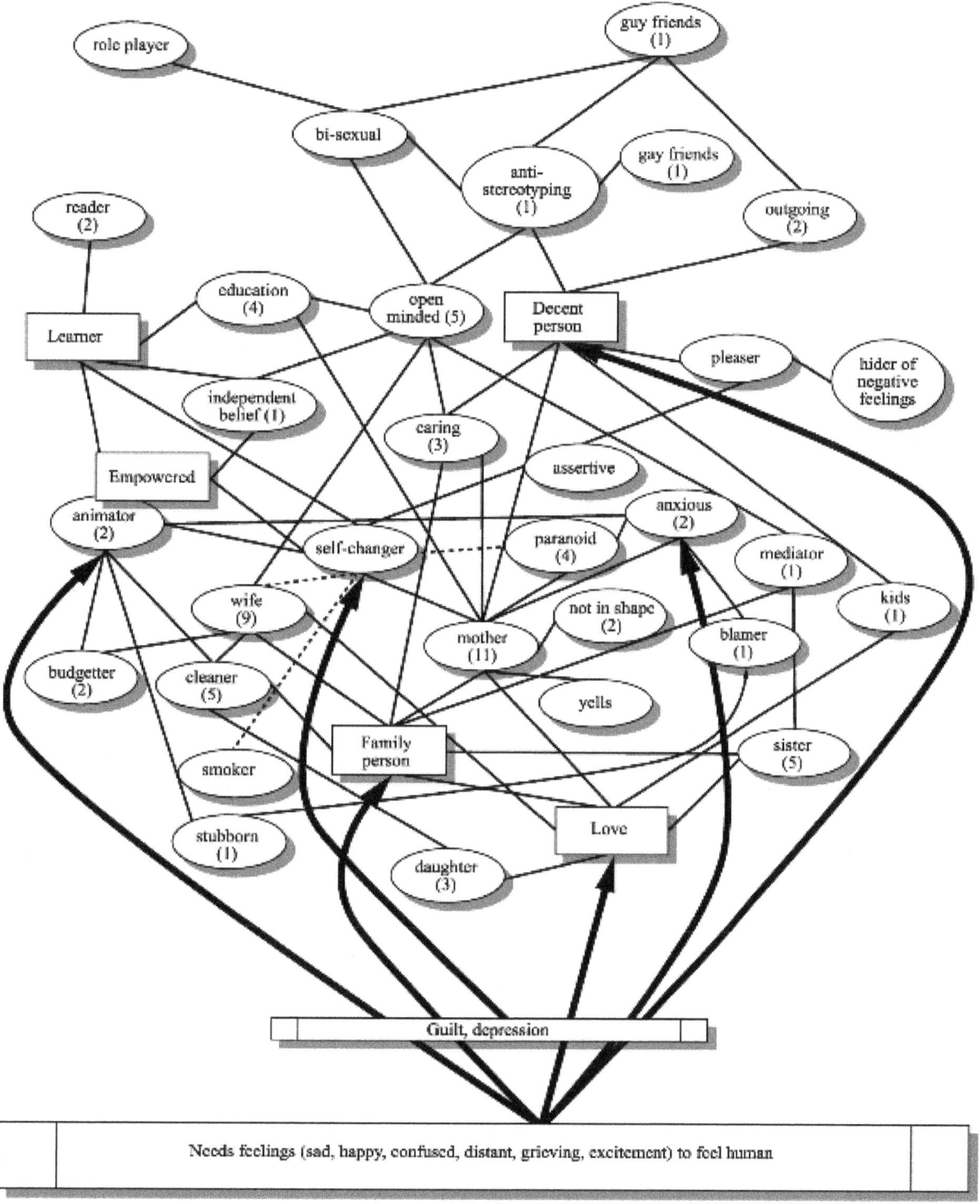

Figure 9: Revised Memetic map of Tina resulting from her second interview (with no further changes resulting from the third interview)

When feelings of depression and guilt are overpowering, Tina reported hiding from others and attempts to generate positive thoughts. Tina admitted during our second interview that she had not always responded to her depression and guilt in this way. She said that as a teenager she would engage in partying and binge drinking in an attempt to remove depressive feelings. In answer to the question, "What made you change?" she answered, "Having kids, you have no choice but to grow up.... The first one fell in my lap, so I didn't plan the first one; he just kind of dropped in my lap; I guess you could say."

Tina's father had a long-term extramarital relationship with a woman that resulted in a half-sister she met by chance when she was a student in high school. Tina explained that learning of her father's infidelity, the manner of meeting her sibling as an adolescent, and her sister's subsequent death had helped shape her worldview:

> The first time that I had to ever deal with death was when my sister died, and that's a big thing that me and my family don't talk about very much 'cause it was an affair and they decided not to tell us about it.... so we grew up in high school, a good 2, 3 years she didn't say anything, and I was hearing impaired, and I seen her (another half sister) at the fair, and she goes "Tina this is your sister," and I thought she said, "This is my sister," so I shook my own sister's hand and walked away from her the first time I met her, just hurt her completely, and my dad was freaking out 'cause he saw the whole thing from afar and he ended up telling me that night that was my actual sister... I got to know her for 2 years and she passed away.

The secrecy and pain associated with her father's promiscuity were followed by several years of "partying" that included binge drinking and illicit drug use. She "sobered up" when she discovered she was pregnant, and she made a decision to raise this child "properly." Reflecting on her experiences, she proposed the idea of an open marriage with her husband providing he did not "sneak around." The crib death of her firstborn led Tina to relapse into a pattern of binge drinking. Tina also credited this experience with the development of overprotectiveness verging on paranoia with respect to the safety of her children. An unplanned pregnancy also led her away from binge drinking on this second occasion. On both occasions, powerful behavioural injunctions associated with motherhood resulted in her choosing a sober lifestyle.

Tina said she quit abusing alcohol when she learned she was pregnant, but she was unable to say why she was different from other women who continued to party despite pregnancy. She only said that she believed children are precious and need to be cared for properly and she attributed that belief to her upbringing. We also discussed changes she had made to her behaviour that allowed her to complete high school. She said she felt responsible to help others, especially children, and that this contributed to her will to change.

She said the act of change in such circumstances connoted decency. As a result of this discussion, we added the meme "self-changer" to her self-map connected to "mother" and "animator." Another centre in Tina's self-map was that of being an animator, defined as someone who gets things done. This meme was only mentioned explicitly in two segments, but it was implied in her self-characterizations as being "stubborn," a "budgeter," and a self-directed learner. The capacity for self-animation implies the interpretive theme "Empowerment."

The "mother" meme is also connected to the interpretive or thematic code "Decent Person." Tina believed that failure in this primary role would threaten her self-identification as a decent person, but the most closely associated meme with this theme is "open-minded." She attributed this quality to her role as mediator in her family of origin because she can see alternative points of view. This quality also leads her to care for and befriend people of minority status and to defend students who have been stereotyped negatively by teachers. Similarly, she defended gays and lesbians in her community. She said being open-minded enhanced her ability to "get along with" her husband, and it contributes to her belief in the importance of education.

Tina attributed the open relationship she has with her husband to her open-mindedness. She said that from her experiences, monogamy is an unrealistic expectation but honesty is. She said that if her husband were to lie and "sneak around," it would "break my heart." She also revealed that she is bisexual, explaining that she had not mentioned that in the first session because she was not sure the counselling psychologist (who was from the same community) would approve. She said that men were generally accepting of her sexuality but that straight women could be "mean and catty." She said she plays a role around straight women. As a result of this new information, we added "bisexual" to her self-map connected to "open-minded," "anti-stereotyping," and "gay friends." We also added "role-player" connected to "bisexual."

The memes for "wife," "daughter," and "cleaner" in Tina's self-map involved the behaviour of cleaning house. Therefore, behaviourally, the three were linked, providing support for each other's presence in Tina's self. The affect associated with both "wife" and "mother" was love, with "love" identified as a unifying theme in Tina's self.

While looking at her initial self-map, Tina mentioned that she is a "yeller." Her children listen to her husband when he talks normally, but she has to yell for them to listen. In response to this information, I added a meme "yeller" to her memetic map, which was attached to "mother." This information could have been added as a descriptor of what it means to be a mother, but the psychologist (LHR) obtained the sense from Tina that this is not how she would define mother.

Tina reported self-change during her second interview. She said she was not as paranoid as she used to be and that she was no longer trying to please everybody. She said she was giving her husband chores at home, and he was helping out with things like laundry and bottle-feeding their baby. These changes, and her new capacity to say "no," allowed her some time to relax, which she realized she had not done before. She had started a part-time job to help out with finances, and this had forced her to get up earlier. Her eldest son told her, "I like it when you have breakfast with me mom," and this led her to realize she had been sleeping in, partly because she had been "a little depressed." She said that she needed to change that aspect of herself; however, she was not always successful. She said she cried during her recent birthday. She had worked "so hard" to make everyone else's birthday special, but she had to buy her own birthday cake and make her own birthday meal.

This new information is consistent with the new meme "self-changer" that we added earlier in this interview, but we also added a new meme labeled "assertive." A dotted line between "self-changer" and "assertive" was used to indicate that she still relapses into non-assertive behaviour, as indicated by her response to the failure of her family to adequately remember her birthday. A meme for "pleaser" was included, indicating Tina takes care of others' needs but often neglects her own, and we attached this meme to "Decent Person," as the core of this tendency to please others is the feeling that she is a good person when she engages in this behaviour.

When invited to share new thoughts or feelings or ways of seeing herself as a result of developing her self-map, Tina replied, "After the first interview, my head was so clear. It was relaxing. I was clear-headed for a good two days after that." She went on to say that she realized that different things made her who she was. In answer to the question, "Does looking at this map of yourself lead you to think of changes that you would want to make to yourself?" Tina replied, "I am going to spend more time on me and not try so hard to make everyone else around me happy." She added that the guilt she feels when she relaxes and the fact that relaxing reminds her of depression inhibit these changes.

During our third session, Tina suggested that the revised map summarized who she is, and that she would not make any changes to it. She said that looking at the map made her realize that guilt and depression were keeping her from feeling a full range of emotions. She decided to fill her prescription for antidepressant medication on the new belief that the antidepressants would allow her to experience a fuller range of emotions than was possible without them. She said the process of self-mapping made her think about things she wanted to change, such as having negative feelings, being a blamer, being paranoid, and being a smoker.

She said she recognizes that she has compulsive behaviours flowing from her childhood experiences that she can change. As an example, Tina reported she has compulsively cleaned the homes of family and friends when visiting. She traced this behaviour to her desire to gain childhood approval from her mother: "When I was little, I used to make my bed, and it would have no creases in it whatsoever, and I used to run over to my mom and show her. I was so proud of myself that I made my bed like that." She said that seeing herself represented in map form allowed her to see the changes she wanted to make and how they would fit with her "true self."

The Complex Self-Map as a Small World Network

Robertson and McFadden (2018) demonstrated that the self-maps produced in this manual are equivalent to graph theory (GT) networks with the self-map memes corresponding to GT vertices, the pair-wise relationships between memes corresponding to GT edges, and the time evolution of the self-mapping diagrams corresponding to GT sequence analysis. The structural difference between figure 9 and figures 7 (Suzie) & 8 (Tina—initial) is that the earlier maps represented cognitive structures representing a conscious representation of a stable self, while figure 9 includes the addition of a largely non-conscious mechanism that quickly shifts attention or focus while appropriating alternate clusters of the self. While the focus of using traditional cognitive behavioural methods involves tracing pathways from memes along edges or links and altering those pathways in some ways, Figure 9 introduced connections from emotional or unconscious centers that trigger a focus on memetic clusters without the necessity of proceeding along linked pathways. We have alternatives to action. We can take the laborious "high road" of methodically thinking about each step in a process or we can intuitively or reactively take the emotional "low road" of responding to stimuli and quickly changing our presentation. Of course, if our objective is to change the self in some ways, we must take use of the cognitive route, but the representation in figure 9 offers a more complete presentation of how the self normally operates as a small-world network.

In their examination of connections in networks using graph theory, Watts and Strogatz (1998) demonstrated that the existence of even a few longer-range connections reduced the minimum path length of networks of self-organizing systems without deleterious effects on local clustering. Put simply, tracing a pathway along short links is both time-consuming and results in an overall longer pathway while the existence of a few long-range "shortcuts" increases the speed of operation and reduces the total distance of movement, making the system more efficient. Drawing on research using fMRI experiments, Bassett and Bullmore (2006) concluded that such a small-world network model provided a powerful approach to understanding the structure and function of human brain systems. Since such a structure combines the stability of linked pathways with the ability to "Leap frog" normal pathways and stimulate distant clusters. From an evolutionary perspective, such a combination of short and long connections would be expected. As Bassett and Bullmore (2006) explained, "Small-world topology is associated with low wiring costs and high dynamical complexity, suggesting that small-world brain network topology could indeed have been selected to optimize the economic problem of cost-effective information processing" (p. 516).

The self-maps discussed in this manual were created by linking memes that shared connotative, affective, or behavioural characteristics. Pathways between memes were mapped, highlighting cognitive and behavioural scripts. These pathways involve a progression through short connecting links simulating conscious thought, but sometimes events, both internal and external, can act as triggers to focus attention on aspects of the self that are removed from the current focus. Missing in figures 7 and 8 is the representation of intuitive and unconscious forces that can lead to thought clusters relatively instantaneously without the necessity of pursuing a series of short connections from a present location. The illustration of a young mother's self in figure 9 added directed edges emanating from her emotional centers pictured at the base of the self-map. Emotions, when triggered, could in turn activate specific clusters of her self-definition centered on themes such as "empowered," "family person," "love," or "anxious." Such emotions, in turn, could be triggered by internal factors such as memories or by external contextual cues. Tina's self-presentation, then, would flow from a combination of local clustering and longer-range thematic and emotive connections.

As we saw, the addition of long-range connections in the example illustrated in figure 9 had an unexpected therapeutic application. Tina had previously refused antidepressant medication because she believed it was important for her to experience all of her emotions. During the course of self-map construction, she realized that her depression and associated guilt had been blocking her ability to feel other emotions. She became amenable to the idea of using medication to remove that blockage. The addition of such long-range connections, whereby specific thematic clusters may be triggered by various psychological mechanisms including emotions, represents a further refinement that can explain comparatively sudden changes in behaviour including the experience of insight.

If the objective of therapy is to change the self in some ways, the maps focusing on memes and meme-pathways may actually be preferable for their relative simplicity of presentation. But the therapist should keep in mind that the self includes mechanisms for interaction with emotive and unconscious factors that can affect presentation. These factors may impede or even limit change.

---

[1] This section is edited from The Evolved Self (2020) pp. 128-132

5

Using Self-mapping to Effect Change

Philosopher Dan Dennett (1995) said that since our minds have finite capacity and since there are more memes within any given culture than could possibly be held by any of the minds within that culture, memes are in an evolutionary struggle for "mind space." Memes, or complexes of memes that replicate successfully, will be passed on within any given culture or between cultures. A simple melody or advertising jingle that comes, unbidden, into our minds is obviously a good replicator. Easily remembered, catchy phrases are ordinarily better replicators than longer reasoned arguments. In war, each side bombards its population with propaganda justifying itself and demonizing the enemy and slogans, if repeated often enough, will be remembered. Dennett (1996) made the controversial suggestion that complexes of memes or memeplexes, are a life form in an ecosystem of human minds called culture whose replicatory interest exists independent of our individual or collective interest as a species. Thriving by convincing us to abandon our sense of reason except for mundane purposes. In this view, complexes of memes come to be accepted as true, beyond the pale of rational discourse, with human beings acting as vectors in promoting certain memeplexes while cancelling, silencing, and otherwise restricting the presentation of alternate views.

If this were the whole story, then we would indeed be a determined species with our presentations completely dependent on genetics and environment. We would be enslaved to our genes and memes with delusions of free will. Fortunately, the evolved self was a cultural adaptation that imbued us with a sense that there's such a thing as objective reality. While the pursuit of objective knowledge has been a boon to science and technology, it also implies that evidence is required to change entrenched views. To the bane of psychotherapists everywhere, clients regularly refuse to replace negative self-descriptors with better ones because the new self-affirmative memes do not feel true. Clients need evidence based on what they understand counts as evidence before such positive change can occur. In a nod to determinism, we are indeed programmed by our genes and our environment, but we are capable of reprogramming ourselves (Robertson, 2017a). The goal of psychotherapy, and the writers of this manual, is to facilitate the empowerment of clients imbued with the critical thinking skills they need to recreate themselves in ways that will lead to fulfilling lives.

Reflections on Maps of the Self

A map is always a simplified representation of the territory mapped; thus, no map can be expected to represent the self of an individual completely; nonetheless, individuals should be able to recognize and identify with their representations. Change occurs to the individual self when memes that were consistent with aspects of the existent self are added to identity or when memes that are no longer consistent with what is felt to be true by the individual are subtracted. Since most of the existent self is left intact while engaging in incremental change, even directed change has an evolutionary flavour.

As we have seen, the utility of the meme, as a concept distinct from percept and idea, rests on the recognition of its referent, connotative, affective, and behavioural dimensions. These dimensions allow for metaphoric attractive force to exist between memes, giving stability to resultant structures. While the use of the meme in this way was efficacious, it was insufficient, as emotive factors not connected to specific memes also make up who we are, and these factors allude to unconscious drives and characteristics. With this realization, we added a "menu of emotions" at the base of self-maps with the implied need to understand what triggers various emotions and what clusters of memes are activated as a result.

The proposition that the self consists of a complex of mutually attractive memes provides an elegant explanation as to why people retain negative or self-defeating aspects of their identities instead of simply constructing newer and better selves. For example, Suzie's initial attempts to change herself by removing "depressed person" from her identity resulted in feelings of instability coupled with suicide ideation and a reflexive retreat into depression. Visualizing herself in memetic map form coincided with her determination to override such protective measures and engage in a process of self-change. The act of situating "depressed person" within a cluster of related memes helped both therapist and client to develop a plan for building a more positive self-construction.

The therapist and client may use self-mapping to identify key structural elements that are weak or missing and dysfunctional elements on which the client may rely for self-definition. Relying on the client's report of resonance with successive co-authored revisions will increase the likelihood that the representation is of sufficient quality. While no map represents a territory perfectly, they allow us to chart a course, and so it is with memetic self-maps. Planned incremental change can take into account groups of memes serving to keep dysfunctional core memes in place. Groups of such memes can be appropriated to support new desired alternatives. Peripheral memes are usually the easiest for the client to remove or replace. Since the map-building activity is necessarily a collaborative exercise between therapist and client, it commends itself to the joint planning of therapeutic alternatives. The dynamic of co-constructing developmental transitions is a way of increasing client self-empowerment and commitment to change. The potential benefits also include enhanced development of collaborative counsellor-client relationships, increased rapport, and a holistic perspective on the self-structure. With such mapping, the client may be able to better understand the consistency of his actions, cognitions, and feelings with an underlying belief system so that a challenging of that belief system can begin.

To help effect change, we look for themes in clusters of memes, and those themes may imply emotionality such as shame, fear, or vulnerability. These themes encompass a kind of script that is enacted when emotions like shame, fear, or vulnerability are triggered in the menu of emotions, the long-range connections mentioned previously. One way to conceptualize this is imagining a client with PTSD. The emotion is triggered and a flashback and/or related behavioural or emotional response is enacted as a result. A cluster of memes has been immediately activated by the emotional trigger. Alternatively, there may be no cluster that is activated when the emotion is triggered. This may be a healthier self, as it may represent processing rather than being stuck or triggered by a past traumatic event that's influenced their perception of self. The steps to interpreting a self-map prepared in the ways commended in this manual include:

1. Identify clusters and patterns with the client. Explore those memes that may be identified as essential to part of who they are.
2. Consider unhelpful aspects that are accepted as part of the self. Explore linked memes that serve to keep those memes as part of the self. Explore how memes supporting maladaptive ones may be refocused or redefined in healthier ways.
3. Explore the contexts that trigger negative clusters or rumination patterns. Co-construct strategies the client may use to avoid those triggers or get out of rumination once it occurs. This is where reframing and building additional pathways out of the rumination cycle occurs.
4. Explore events that precipitated the inclusion of unhelpful memes and what they believe was different about themselves prior to those occurrences.
5. Explore the self-map for evidence of the seven core elements identified as characteristic of a healthy, functioning modern self. Consider activities or homework to facilitate the development of any missing elements.

Seven Core Elements of the Modern Self

Our primate ancestors had developed a form of the self when they learned mirror recognition several million years ago. A more developed self was in evidence 50,000 years ago when our ancestors developed funeral rituals and art in the form of cave paintings. The modern self with its qualities of constancy, distinctness, volition, productivity, intimacy, social interest, and remembering/reflecting appeared as recently as three thousand years ago (Robertson, 2020). Let us reflect on each of these elements in turn.

1. Constancy: This is the feeling that we remain the same person over time despite changes to our physical features, abilities, and worldview. Without this particular quality, we would be unable to place ourselves in past remembered events or possible futures.
2. Uniqueness: This is the view that we are a unique person separate from all others despite shared qualities. If we were identical to another person in all ways, we would still have the sense of being distinct in some undefined way.
3. Volition: This is the sense that we have the power to enforce our will. People with this quality believe that they can affect their future in positive or negative ways and thus are responsible, to some extent, for their own well-being.

4. Productivity: People with healthy selves believe they are contributing through their own efforts. Payment for work is evidence of the value of such contribution, but whether an activity is productive is ultimately defined by the individual.
5. Intimacy: Although we are individuals, we need to feel closeness to a defined set of others. This could include a marriage partner, family members, or close friends.
6. Social Interest: This is the feeling that we are benefiting our families, communities, or societies in some ways. It is a sense of connection and contribution to the common good.
7. Remembering/Reflecting: This is the act of thinking about past events in which we place ourselves in the role of protagonist and consider other possible outcomes, especially as to how we may have affected those outcomes.

Students of psychology will note that the first three elements on this list were first identified by William James in the late 19th century (James, 1890). The following three elements—productivity, intimacy, and social interest – were identified by Alfred Adler (1927/1957). The last element, remembering, is necessary as it places the self in time and has an emotional connotation that affects perception; it is a necessary function to notice and effect change. In addition to these seven cognitive elements, the self also includes heritable psychological characteristics such as the "Big Five" (extroversion, neuroticism, openness to experience, agreeableness, and conscientiousness) and triggering emotions such as that which may be generated by the amygdala. These are not part of the cognitive portion of the self but are important determinants of the self and its functioning. Whether or not the clinician chooses to place these primordial elements in the map will be determined by client needs. One way this may be incorporated is by including a menu of emotions, which, in the case of Tina (Figure 9), was needed to deal with her conceptualization of emotional wholeness and was placed at the bottom of her self-map.

The seven elements of the self may be stated by the client or inferred. Figure 10 is the self-map of a man in his 50s who was troubled by the possibility that he lacked one of those elements.

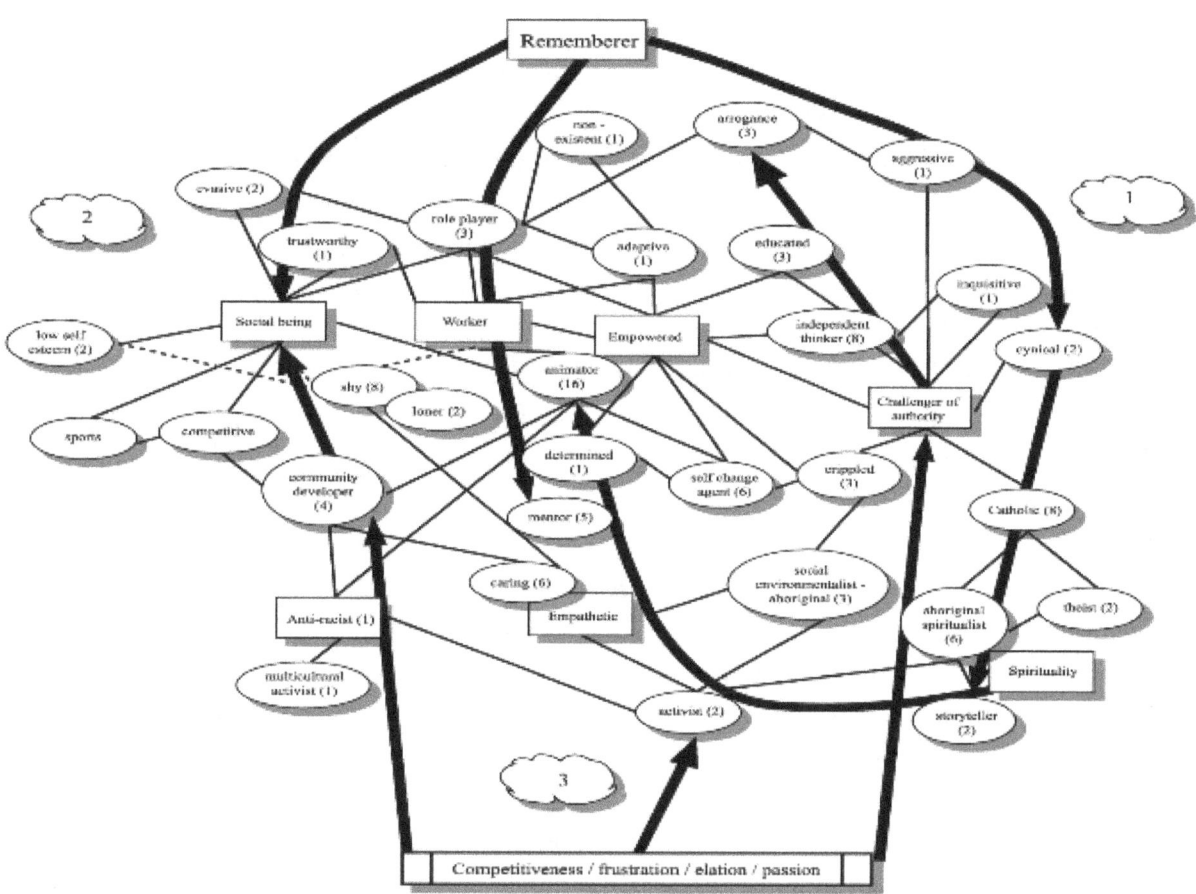

Figure 10: Amended memetic self-map of JohnB following his second mapping interview

JohnB was a volitional individual beginning in his early years as a challenger of authority. He later developed a successful career in management where he trained and supervised numerous staff. He was productive both in his work and in his contribution to community organizations. He had few close friends but developed intimacy with his wife and his son. He displayed social interest by helping people through volunteer activities, through sports, and by conducting anti-racist teachings to non-aboriginal people.

The bottom of JohnB's self-map features the most common emotions he felt that would trigger presentations drawn from various parts of his self, but it also depicts "Rememberer" as a theme. His memories would also trigger a focus on various aspects of his self, most commonly cynicism, mentorship, and his social being.

JohnB lacked a sense of his own distinctness. His self-map is marked by three temporal clusters. Cluster 1 marks his self as a youth centred on the theme "challenger of authority." JohnB was introverted and awkward socially, so he played a role to develop a career in management. He also acted a part to develop his social skills (cluster 2), and he admitted that sometimes he would refuse to answer the telephone or doorbell because he was more comfortable being alone. In time, JohnB adopted Aboriginal spirituality, which formed the basis of his third self-cluster.

JohnB's progression through his major self-clusters resulted from maturation coupled with fortuitous life events. His early self-definition flowed from contradictions he interpreted as hypocrisies that led him to challenge both parental and church authority. In high school he befriended a non-Christian aboriginal girl who, in his words, "was as entitled to go to heaven as I was." He also excelled in sports despite having been born with a clubfoot and learned that he could succeed on the strength of an iron will. Social skills did not come easy to him, but he used his will to role-play success socially and at work, and this defined his second major self-cluster. He found work in an aboriginal community and married a woman from that community. He concluded that Aboriginal spirituality was closer to the original teachings of Christianity than the Christianity he had been taught as a child, but he still had problems with identity. He had the sense that he had been playing roles all through his life and that he did not know who he was outside of the roles he played. He worried that in some sense he might not exist, and he needed to root himself in traditions that he could identify as his. With respect to the seven components of the self we have identified, JohnB lacked a sense of his own uniqueness and continuity.

It has been our experience that client resistance to therapy can be caused by a sense that if they change who they are, they will cease to be themselves, similar to the experience of JohnB. The act of self-mapping gives them the visual grounding that they will continue to be the same person while changing some aspects of who they are.

The various schools of therapy may be thought of as emphasizing combinations of the seven structural elements reviewed in this manual. Cognitive-behavioural therapy has stressed volition, activity, and thinking. Adlerian Psychotherapy (Dinkmeyer et al., 1979; Maniacci et al., 2014) adds intimacy and social interest to the mix. Other therapies focus more specifically on emotion or remembered narratives. All therapies recognize the uniqueness of the individual, but most do not elevate this element to their central focus.

Figure 11 reproduces the self-map of a man in his early 20s with Asperger's Syndrome. The paucity of memes in his self-map flows from his difficulty in generating a detailed self-description. As would be expected with a person with his condition, there is little in his self-map related to family, intimacy, or social interest. "Son" appears, but his meme for son is different from most. He said he was a son but the emotion attached to this was appreciation that he was allowed to stay at his father's place. "Environmentalist" appears as a meme but the interest here was in reading and learning about it. He could recite numerous statistics related to global warming and environmental change, but he did not exhibit an emotional commitment to maintaining the environment.

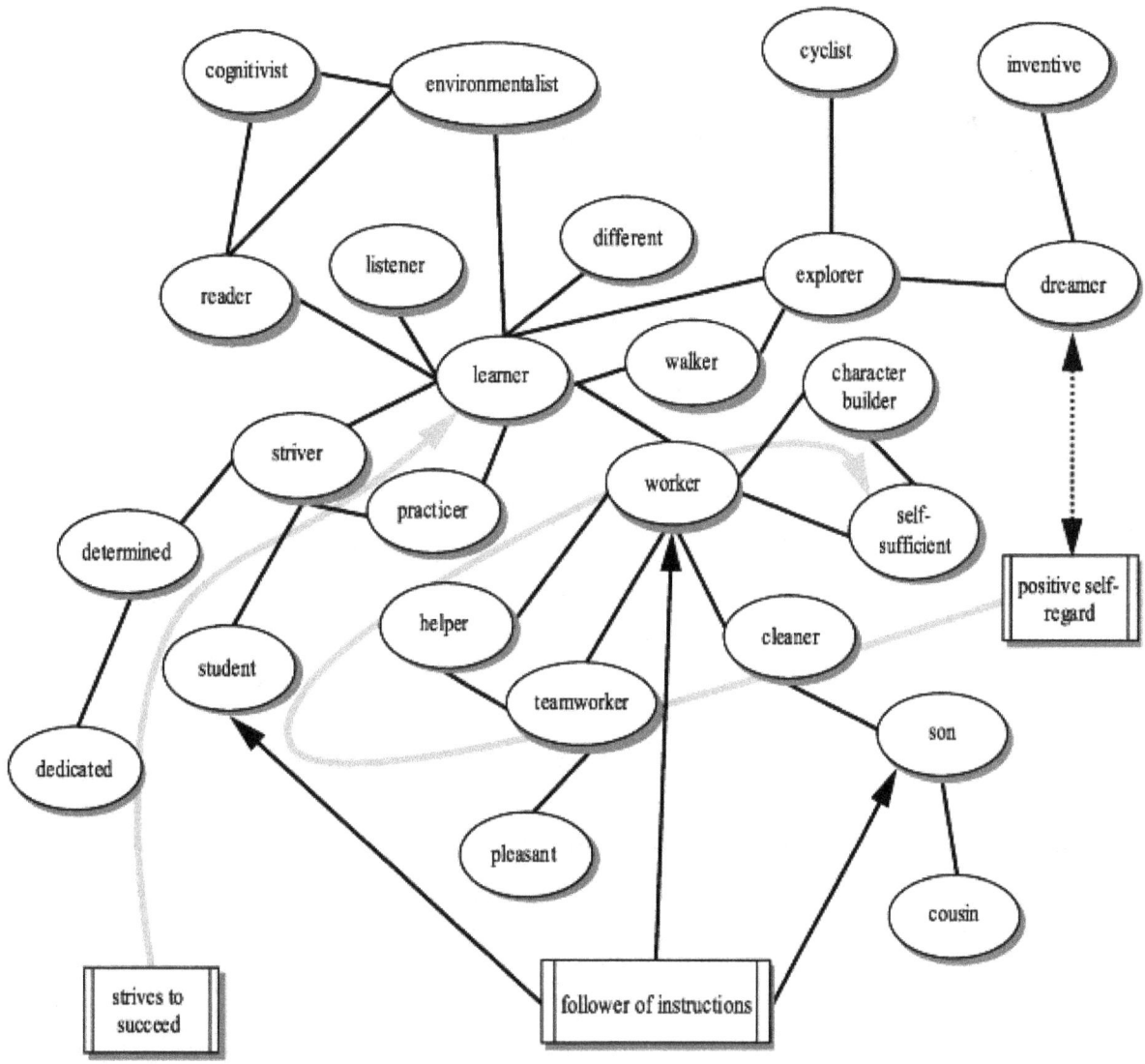

Figure 11: The self-map of a young man with Asperger's Syndrome

His answers to questions were overly concrete. He defined himself as a learner on the basis of attending a post-secondary institution, but he had little interaction with his fellow students and when they attempted to interact with him, he would fail to respond in kind. Nonetheless, he viewed himself as having many friends among his classmates. He viewed himself as a student, worker, and son because he had followed the instructions of his father to engage in these roles. He defined himself as a dreamer because he had dreams while he slept thus illustrating the importance of knowing the client's affect, connotations, and behaviours associated with each referent word or phrase.

While counselling may focus on problem solving, psychotherapy is about self-change. The self may be thought of as a theory each of us has of who we are. Each meme is a proposition linked to other such propositions in logical and emotive ways. With new information it should be possible to construct better self-theories. We have an impulse to seek evidence that will either confirm or extend our self-definitions.

Psychotherapists continuously confront confirmation bias when helping clients construct better selves. Clients have their own habitual ways of defining what constitutes evidence and we need to explore and extend those definitions with them. Some individuals with negative self-images resist feedback because they fear confirmation of what they already fear is true. The challenge of therapists is to provide objectively defensible rationale for exploring self-enhancing change in a safe and nurturing place. The core of the modern self is the idea that there is an objective reality, and psychotherapists are in the business of helping our clients explore that reality through hypothesis testing and rational discourse. We teach clients emotional intelligence and rational observation and discourse.

While the self may not be purely a cognitive structure, it is possible to bring more of that structure into conscious awareness. The client may be relatively unaware of personal psychological characteristics such as intelligence, kindness, shyness, or other dispositional qualities that may be true but unacknowledged.

Emotions may be a window to the unconscious. For example, in working with aboriginal clients exhibiting Residential School Syndrome, the lead author observed examples of rage in contexts where even anger would be unwarranted (Robertson, 2006). Triggers to such episodes often reveal a connection to past events that counted as evidence in support of currently held dysfunctional worldviews. A common example of this frequently seen in therapy are those who fear rejection to such an extreme that they assume they are being rejected and respond as such without adequate evidence, leading to a self-fulfilling prophecy. Self-mapping may be an aid in making these unconsciously held worldviews conscious. Since self maps, as constructed here, are based on what is or may be consciously known, they allow us to explore deeper and heretofore unrecognized interpretations of selfhood. In all of the examples, the act of self-mapping led to reflective thought on the part of the client or participant exploring those deeper interpretations.

We witnessed this process at work in the example of Suzie in Chapter 3. The new core meme "human rights" focused on the element missing in her self-social interest. But she needed to change her community to support her new self. Once a self has been defined, that person is maintained from selected memories supported by expectations of consistency and continuity from a surrounding community. Thus, an alcoholic who successfully completes a residential treatment program may still be considered an alcoholic by his community with a resultant increase in the probability of relapse. Therapists attempt to combat memetic pressure resisting self-change by temporarily occupying the role of significant other and by mobilizing resources, both internal and external, in support of the change process. The successful therapist acknowledges and buttresses those aspects of the individual's self-definition that tend to support the desired change and assists the client in re-defining his surrounding community to give increased prominence to those supportive of the change effort.

Equally important, therapists also need to acknowledge aspects of the client's self not in need of change that support a sense of constancy. The client needs to feel that in some important sense the person coming out of therapy is still the same person who entered it. Seeing oneself in map form placing the desired change in perspective assists this sense of constancy. Successful change requires support from memes already existent within the self, and such change may be viewed as part of an evolutionary process.

Empowerment and self-efficacy [1]

When we consider the factors we as therapists hope to build in clients for them to enact their own change, we must look at empowerment and self-efficacy. The Cambridge Dictionary [2] defines empowerment as "the process of gaining freedom and power to do what you want or to control what happens to you" and self-efficacy as "a person's belief that they can be successful when carrying out a particular task." To demonstrate how memetic mapping can support clients in building these factors, we will explore the case of Olivia and what changes she made in her life as a result of experiencing the mapping process.

"Olivia," an aboriginal [3] woman in her thirties, was on medical leave for trauma after having been raped by a friend with whom she had spent a night of drinking. Police decided there was insufficient evidence to lay charges. She was subject to verbal assaults from family members of the alleged perpetrator in a remote northern community and experienced daily anxiety attacks. Treatment included psycho-education about anxiety, progressive relaxation, visualization involving symptom reversal, positive self-affirmations, and meaning-making. She was able to resume work within six weeks; however, she noted that she had a history of alcoholism and self-defeating behaviours, and she asked that counselling be continued for self-development. Using the "forty persons" method for identifying memes, Olivia listed her defining roles, positive attributes, negative attributes, and beliefs. Memes identified from these lists were used to co-construct the self-map in Figure 12.

This self-map includes three clusters labelled Spiritual/Fitness, Social, and Imperfect. Olivia associated outdoor activities such as fishing, hunting, hiking, and snowshoeing with spiritual, meditative, and mystical processes with the result that the themes labelled "Spiritual" and "Fitness" are linked. A connotation linked interconnectedness to her environmentalist, outdoorsy, god-believing, and spiritualist memes. She also saw herself as interconnected with her large extended family and this cognitive path leads to a cluster labelled "Social Person." Her family was central to her social self, and she had learned from them to be "supportive," which she defined as "doing for others."

If she felt imposed upon or put upon by supporting others, a connotative meaning led to the self-critical, "oversensitive" meme, which, in turn, led to depression and anxiety, the core of her "Imperfect" self cluster. This cluster was made more debilitating by the presence of a self-defining perfectionist meme, but that meme also led to self-directed learning that, in turn, could stimulate her sense of adventure, taking her out of that cluster.

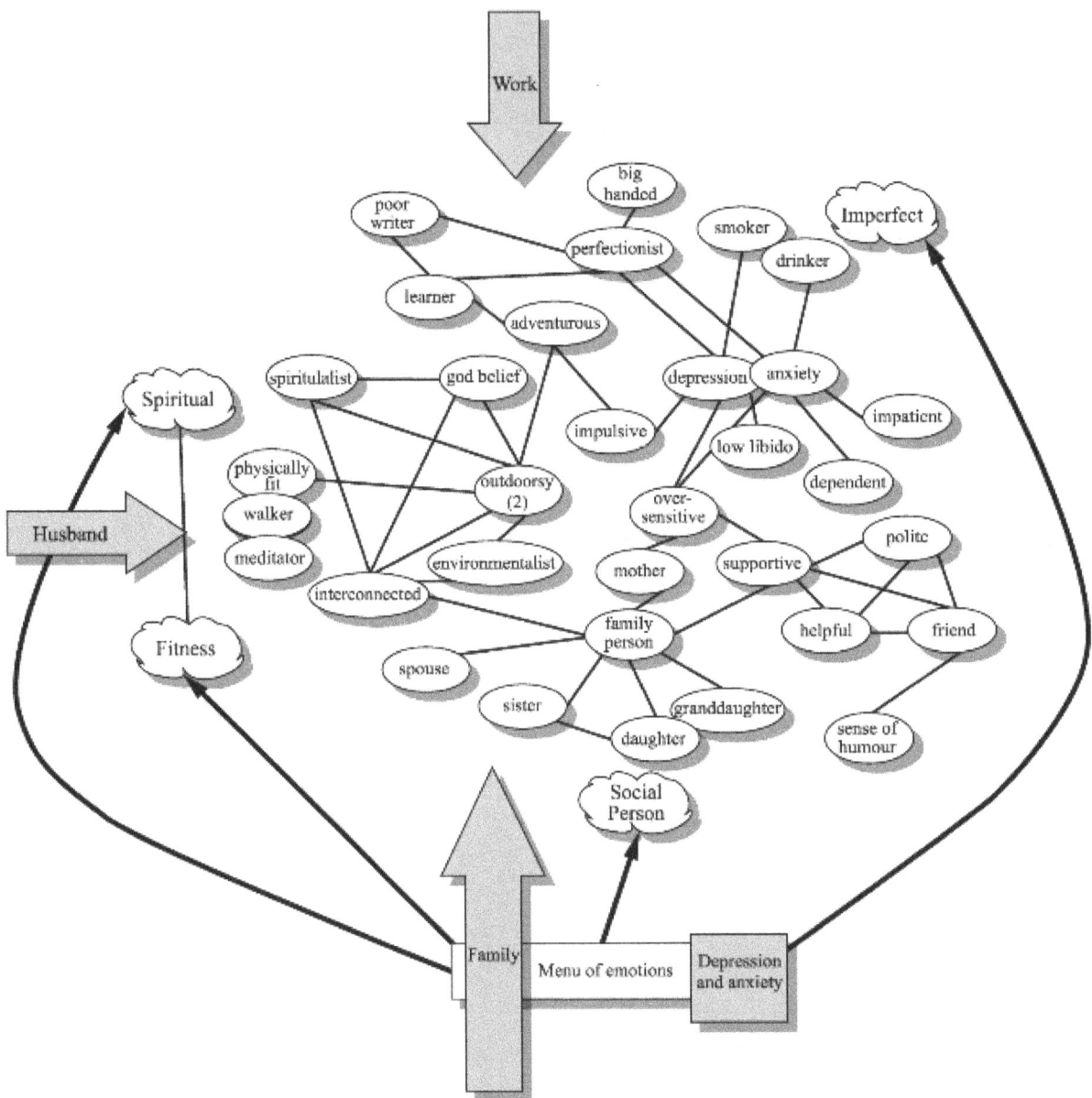

Figure 12: Initial self-map of Olivia displaying memes, external influences and emotions

Olivia's "Imperfect Self" became associated with patterns of rumination and binge drinking. The bar at the bottom of Olivia's self-map represents a menu of emotions that, if triggered, could shift the subject's focus to a particular cluster. Clinical depression and anxiety distinct from her cognitive representations of the same name are also pictured here. Whereas in Tina's self-map (Figure 9) depression and guilt were pictured as blocking other emotions and deactivating an empowering meme; in this case, depression and anxiety are pictured as triggers activating Olivia's "Imperfect Self" cluster. Her family, spouse, and work associates were presented as being supportive and are represented in Figure 12 with broad green arrows with external origins.

After reflecting on the effect that alcohol had on her life, Olivia committed to not drinking to excess, and this was defined as a maximum of two drinks per social occasion. With the successful application of this rule, the meme "drinker" was changed to "social drinker." Olivia's husband continued in a pattern of heavy drinking that had been the pattern for both of them previously. Olivia initially attempted to accommodate him by being "the designated driver" and by taking care of him. She reported, however, that he was a "mean drunk," verbally attacking her for trying to change, criticizing her housework, and accusing her of infidelity. He began checking her e-mail, social media sites, and cell phone while sober. At a counselling session, she announced that she had left her spouse the week before and had moved into a small, unfinished family cabin. She appeared positive about this new development and scored low on the North American Depression Inventory. As this improvement was maintained, we were able to remove "depression" from her self-map. When challenged to state what she would do with her increased free time, she looked at her map and said "photography," which she linked to "learner," "outdoorsy," and "environmentalist." She also linked it to "sensitive" because it was from that space she hoped to gain perceptiveness and perspective. "Sensitive" represented a reframe of the meme "Oversensitive." "Oversensitive" had been a word used by her family of origin to describe her complaints, often leading to depression, after she stopped being "supportive" by failing to do things for them. These changes are represented in Figure 13.

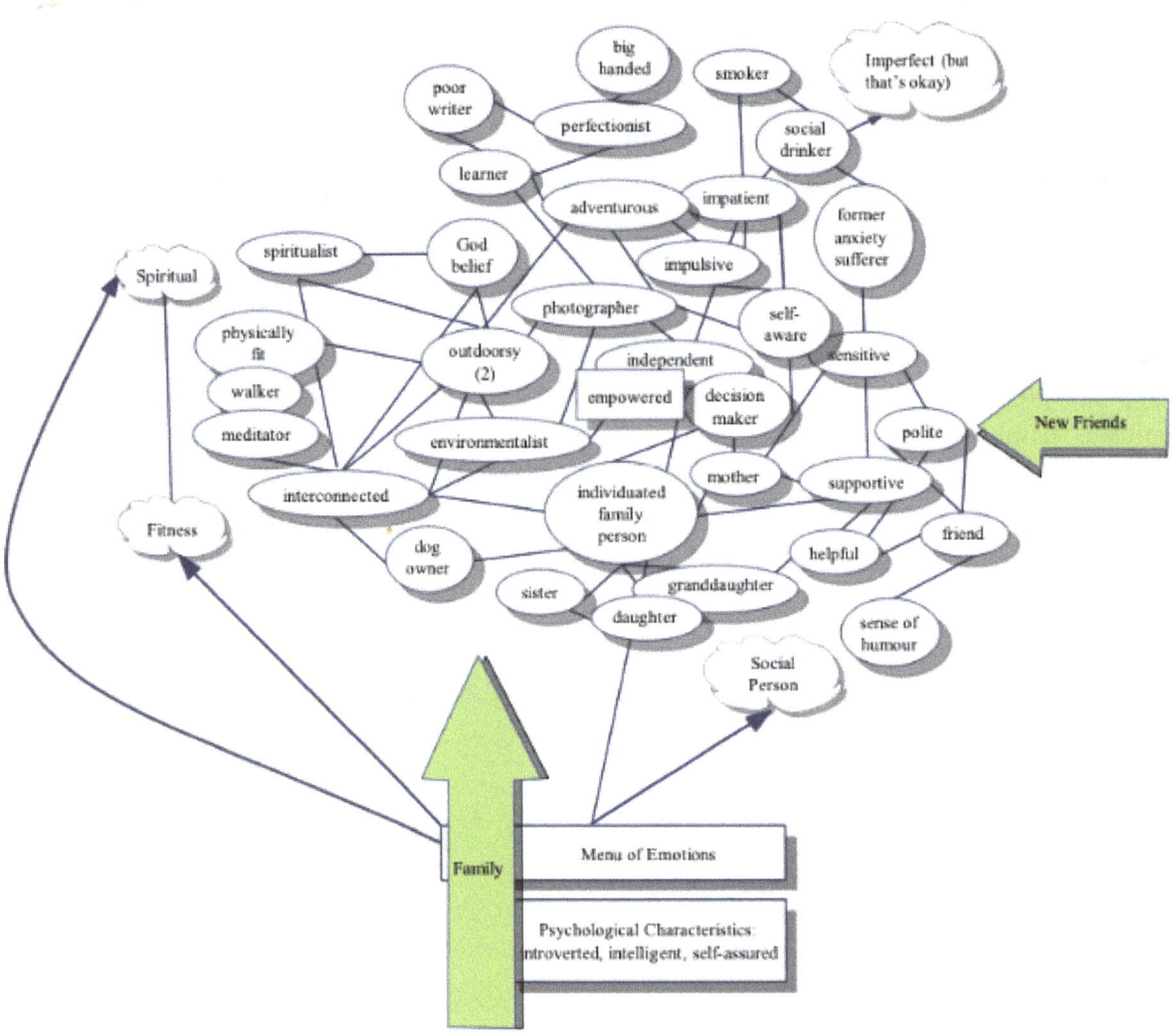

Figure 13: Olivia's self-map as co-constructed immediately prior to the termination of therapy

Olivia reported that she no longer felt respected at work and that she was not given the information or latitude to do her job properly. She also found her family, particularly her mother, to be invasive and controlling. She came to realize that she had changed, and actions that had been perceived to be supportive 6 months earlier were now felt to be restrictive. With the support of her family, she moved to another community, found a new job, and began professional training in photography.

Our final session included a review of her self-map to reflect any further changes in her self-definition. She added, "dog owner," reflecting the increased importance her pet came to have in her life. "Family person" became "individuated family person," reflecting her continued love for her parents while enforcing newly established boundaries. She offered the insight that being "sensitive" had led to her becoming "self-aware," and that, in turn, fuelled her newfound sense of independence and decision-making. This combination of independent decision-making and self-awareness led her to set boundaries with respect to her family, pursue her interests in photography and environmentalism, and redefine her role as a mother.

Olivia's post-therapeutic self is pictured as having an increased number of internal connections allowing her to move between cognitive clusters, thereby reducing the tendency to ruminate. For example, she could focus on photography or her sense of empowerment in moving away from a debilitating sense of imperfection or inadequacy. We explored those psychological qualities that helped her to revise who she was so effectively. She said she was introverted (which for her connoted self-reflection) and self-assured. I also added "intelligent" to a list of psychological characteristics even though that list was never intended to be a complete listing of attributes.

This case study demonstrated an ability by the client to take charge of her own treatment. Not only did she complete commitments made in therapy, for example, successfully becoming a social drinker and taking up photography, but she successfully initiated actions before discussing them in therapy. She decided, for example, that she needed to move on from her husband after having unsuccessfully implemented a plan to keep their relationship viable. When she determined that her family and employer were failing to recognize her new resolve, thereby effectively supporting her old self, she moved to a new community. Her example illustrates a tendency we have observed that self-mapping often empowers clients to take charge of their own treatment.

---

[1] This case study of "Olivia" first appeared in the Journal of Counselling and Psychotherapy: Robertson, L. H. (2016). Self-mapping in counselling: Using memetic maps to enhance client reflectivity and therapeutic efficacy. Canadian Journal of Counselling and Psychotherapy, 50(3), 332-347.

[2] See https://dictionary.cambridge.org/dictionary/english/empowerment

https://dictionary.cambridge.org/dictionary/english/self-efficacy

[3] The word "aboriginal" is used here as an adjective and is, therefore, not capitalized. The authors are aware that some people treat the word as a proper noun but then defining the term as a racial or national group becomes problematic as illustrated by the following sentence: "Both the Aboriginals (coll: Aboriginees) and Torres Strait Islanders are aboriginal to Australia."

6

Understanding Transition and Non-Transition

in Self Development

Each person's map is a unique representation of who they are at a given point, but the self changes over time. While there are many patterns to be identified in the mapping process, we need to also explore how life events lead to meaningful change and how there may be whole parts or clusters of the self that are not integrated with the rest. We need to also recognize when individuals consciously or subconsciously hide part of their self during the mapping process.

Life transitions can have a robust effect on the self, causing substantial change. Life transitions are changes in an individual's life that require them to adapt and adjust. Marriage, divorce, losing a job, or starting a new career are examples of events that can lead to changes in how people define themselves. In transitions, it is common for people to experience fear, anxiety, excitement, and self-doubt caused by the unknown. Transitions are an unavoidable human experience and provide therapists insights into how clients cope with change and make meaning from events. Such information can be used to inform the mapping process and often clarifies the connections between memes. The stories clients share of transitional periods are important to the mapping process.

It is important to identify the false self when understanding life transitions. Here we explore what results when clients are not forthcoming about all aspects of themselves or are presenting in a way they believe is more desirable or serves a purpose in therapy. A false self may be unconscious, as when individuals subconsciously repress or deny part of who they are even while the repressed part continues to affect their emotions and behaviour in some ways. Therapists need to exercise caution when invoking the notion of a "false self" since honestly held self-representations that others may deem as "false" may represent who they are at any given point in time. The last concept explored in this section is that of mini-selves. Such mini-selves are represented as distinct clusters that are largely separate from the rest of the self. It is possible the last two concepts may be influenced by additional issues such as personality disorders; however, more research into this is needed.

Examples of Transitioning Selves

Feelings of resonance and constancy were enhanced by self-maps reflecting childhood and adult transitions. This recognition of prior transitional change suggests a fluidity that contrasts with a view of the self as unchanging. In cross-cultural research into the structure of the self (Robertson, 2020), each participant was able to recall such transitions, and those events, combined with their interpretations of them, were relayed to the researcher in the form of narratives or remembered self-defining stories. Often these transitions involved overcoming opposition or disadvantage. JohnB, who was born with a clubfoot, refused to accept this physical limitation:

> I think that was quite critical in who I became to be because I wasn't supposed to play and I wasn't supposed to walk well, and I think there was the determination to do it.... I'd come home from school and basically.... because you're not supposed to be doing that, how many times are you gonna hurt yourself? And I think it just gave me more determination to do it. (Robertson, 2020 p. 216)

JohnB was able to trace the competitiveness found in his self-map to his childhood reaction to disability. He used this determination to overcome shyness and develop academic success. The parenting style in which he was raised also influenced his development. He described his parents as emotionally abusive, with this emotional memory triggering negative, even vengeful reactions toward people he perceived as arrogant and authoritative. Cognitive change proved to be easier than emotional change. JohnB credited his experience of moving to northern Saskatchewan with changing from being a conservative Catholic to a more liberal and accepting individual. He noted that in his adopted community, "There are aboriginal, Metis; extremes of wealth.... One can play on a team with a cop, a drug dealer, aboriginals, executives - and they all get along" (Robertson, 2020, p. 216). He was primed for cross-cultural change by the childhood experience of having a non-Christian, non-Caucasian friend who was, in his opinion, as entitled to go to Heaven as those in the congregation in which he was raised.

Conversely, the self feels permanent. To the angst of counsellors since the beginning of the profession, the self, in its striving for continuity, resists change. Self-mapping may aid in engaging the client's commitment to change by illustrating the structural integrity of the whole, thus satisfying the client's need for constancy. By referencing transitional events illustrating the ability to overcome early maladaptive self-definitions, we help empower further beneficial change. JohnB used the same determination that led him to overcome his childhood physical disability to change early self-defining memes of "extremely shy" and "social idiot." In another example, "Judy[1]" credited a job as a carhop with the incidental effect of curing the extreme shyness she felt as a youth, although she continued to be cautious in her presentation style. Reflective self-analysis resulted in her understanding that this shyness led her to appear stern when she was not, and she was able to modify her presenting behaviours to better reflect the person she felt she was inside.

Self-change is facilitated by the opinions of significant others. "Magdelynn" credited her drive toward overachievement with accompanying self-criticism to being the oldest in her sib-line, but she also reported that her motorcycle accident, that had left her wheelchair bound, had resulted in more acceptance of environmental determinism. She said she had little or no control over externally generated events but that "somehow everything eventually works out" in what she labeled a "Forest

Gump life." She was aided by a newfound curiosity leading her to want to explore where such a life would take her. This change, however, happened after the intervention of a valued friend:

> I was upset a lot and quite suicidal, I guess, until one of my friends, a new friend that I made, who was (also) in a chair, he was like, "You were an athlete before; you can still be an athlete," and I was like, "What are you talking about? That don't make any sense to me." He said, "You have the heart and drive and determination to be as active as you were, and you still have that. You just have to find a different sport. You have to find a sport that works for you now. (Robertson, 2020 p. 217)

According to Magdelynn, her friend had taken liberties with the word "athlete" in this quote. Although she had played intramural women's hockey, she had never defined herself as an athlete. But now, with her latest "five-year life plan" in tatters due to her accident, she "went with the flow" and joined a wheelchair basketball team. She said she was initially driven by the anger she felt "at life" after her debilitating accident, but that after a year she found herself on the national women's basketball team. At that point she added a meme for "athlete" to her self-map, which, in turn, had been built on the meme "gimp" pictured in figure 14.

Magdelynn reported that she had always been an achiever and an active competitor and that she felt that life was over, literally, her life was over, after her accident. Threats to the self are felt to be existential. What she discovered, however, was that her disability could be incorporated into her identity while maintaining a sense of continuity. Another less noticed transition was also occurring at this time. Memes for "flexible" and "rigid" both appeared in her self, but both cannot be simultaneously true, and this introduced an element of instability. Madelynn's "Forest Gump" metaphor referenced a deliberate strategy of favouring her "flexible" meme. Transition for her meant acceptance that she could not determine her future, but she was in control of how she played the game.

UNDERSTANDING TRANSITION AND NON-TRANSITION — | 57 |

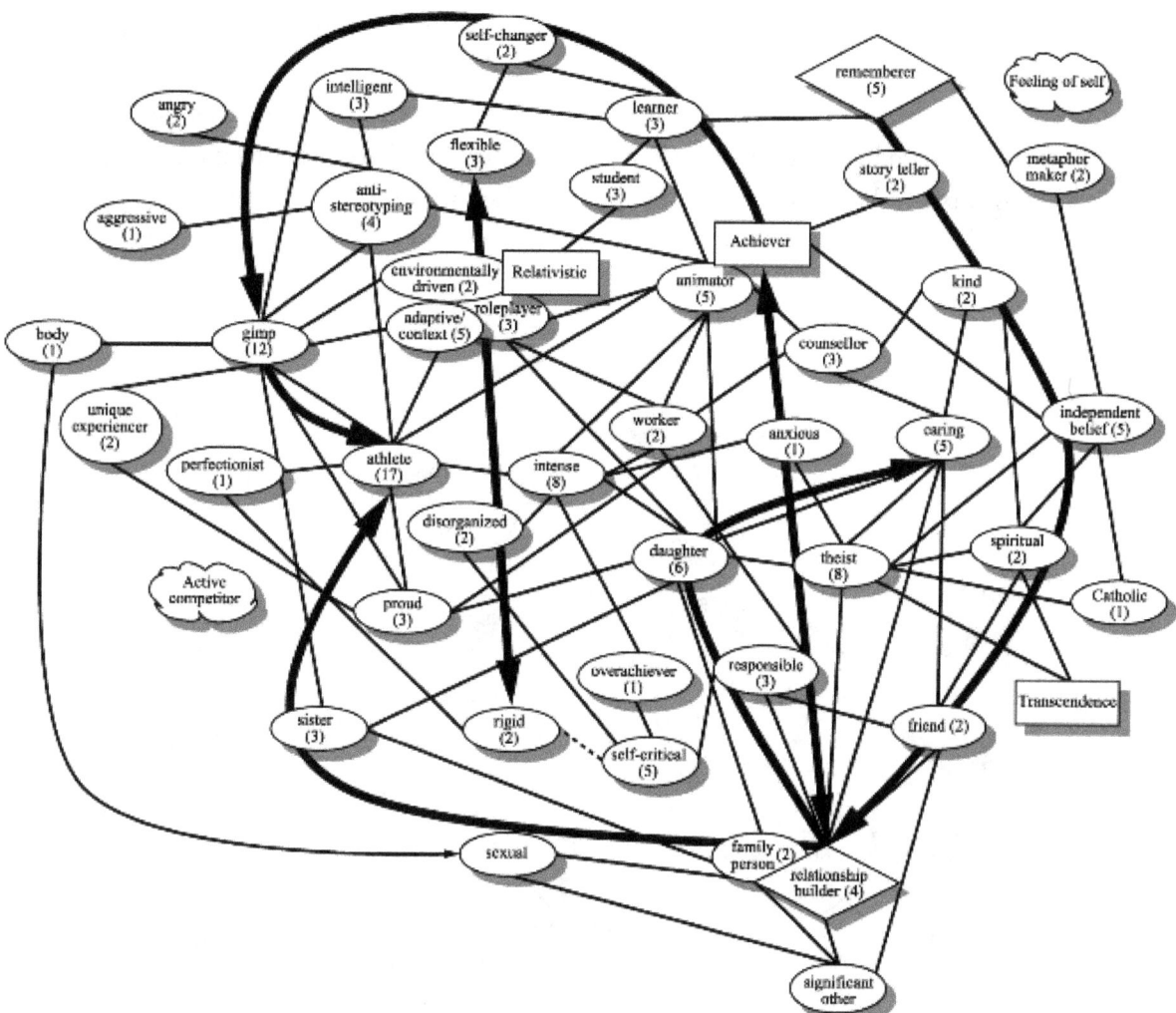

Figure 14: Magdalynn's self – Athlete via wheelchair

A suggestion from a significant other also led "Brent" to experience a planned transitional change. He had believed himself to be someone who lacked academic ability due to a history of educational failure. Subsequent events were interpreted from that internalized frame, and he avoided academic challenges while maintaining a compensating interest in sports. With the encouragement of a swimming coach, who was also a university professor, he began teaching swimming. In effect, he was experimenting with a "poor learner" meme contained in his theory of self. That experimentation led to successful experiences first as a swimming instructor and then as a cycling coach, which, in turn, led to a revised theory of himself as a person of intelligence who can teach. This led him to add "teacher" and "student" his self-map pictured in Figure 15.

In memetic terms he replaced a "poor learner" meme with a "learner" meme. He enrolled in a faculty of education, but his subsequent academic success led to a mini-existential crisis in which his need for self-constancy was threatened. Instead of choosing the understanding that he developed academic acumen to become a competent learner, Brent chose to believe he had always been a competent learner, but external factors had interfered with previous attempts at academic success. Such an interpretation preserves a sense of constancy but invites externalized blame.

Brent blamed his parents for his previously low academic self-esteem, and he cultivated memories of their disapproval when he failed to meet their expectations. He also cultivated memories, attributing both his frugality and his sense of empowerment to their influence.

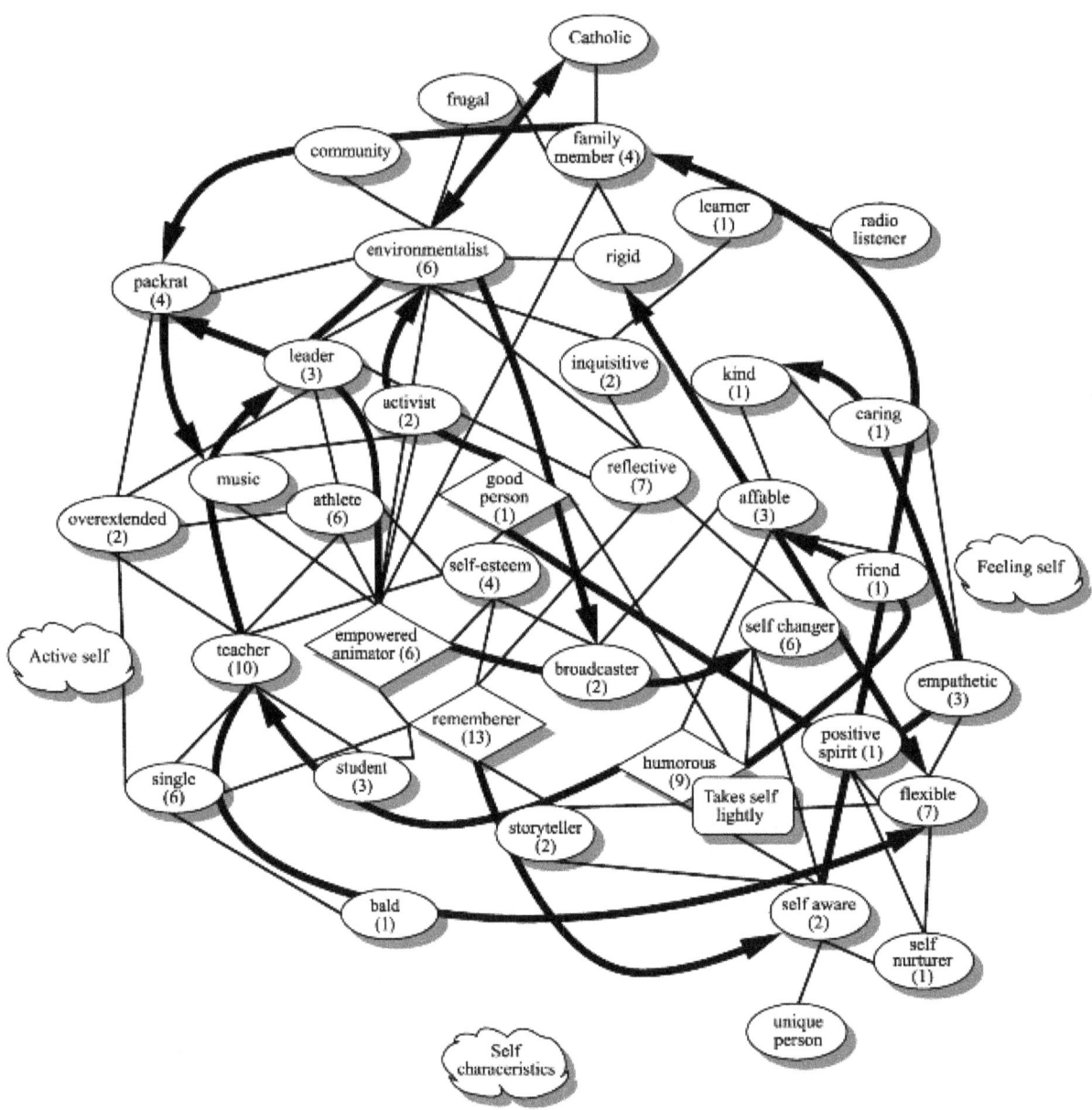

Figure 15: Self Map of "Brent" after he identified as a teacher and student.

Brent's "frugal" meme included what he termed "pack rat" behaviours. He saved everything from newspapers that he had read to clippings from haircuts that he had (catalogued and dated). His motivation was not that these items might be useful someday but that they triggered memories that he might otherwise forget. "Rememberer" is pictured as both a theme and a meme in Figure 15 and was coded for more segments (13) than any other meme following our initial interview. His house was so filled with memorabilia that he did not have room for ordinary furniture. He decided it was time to change his packrat behaviours after a woman he had been dating ended the relationship because she did not feel comfortable at his house, which was cold and did not have a couch. He then resolved to reduce his packrat behaviours and discovered that if he took pictures of saved items, then he could throw them away, thus allowing himself to make his house more visitor-friendly.

Brent also decided to become less rigid in his social interactions with other people, and as with Magdelynn's self, pictured in figure 14, there was tension pictured between memes labeled "rigid" and "flexible." It is our experience that clients who use the name "rigid" as a referent are often on their way to becoming less rigid. People not wanting to change this aspect of themselves would more likely use a referent word or phrase suggesting the same behaviours are "reasonable expectations." Should a client embrace rigidity on principle, then it is not likely that they would also embrace a meme for "flexibility." While in theory a meme can exert attractive or repellent pressure on other memes, in the practice of self-construction, memes that are repelled by other memes are simply not there – they do not form part of the person's self-identity.

Two other memes present in opposition to each other in Brent's self – environmentalist and Catholic. By the time the lead author saw Brent, he had been an environmental activist for over a decade with the sense that his actions contribute to saving the planet. He explained that the Catholic Church had not been supportive of environmentalism and that as a result he had become non-practising. Thus, we find the Catholic meme on the edge of Brent's self kept in place only in terms of remembered upbringing. This arrangement destabilized after graduation and he had to declare his Catholicism to get a teaching position with a publicly funded separate school board. Brent opined that his interviewers probably suspected that his explanation of his Catholicism was not sincere, but in any case, the act of resuscitating a once dormant Catholicism gave him considerable emotional angst.

Transitional change will often produce emotional angst. Brent maximized his sense of constancy in the midst of change by keeping the referent words while changing the connotative, emotional, and behavioural meanings implied by those referents. These are behavioural changes without the necessity of change to the self. While one might expect that sustained behavioural change will lead to changes in self-definition, the need for self-constancy can lead to the retention of old memes even after the behaviours supporting them have ceased. As with people who continue to define themselves as alcoholics years after they stopped abusing the drug, Brent's need for self-constancy led him to continue to define himself as a packrat after he had stopped exhibiting packrat behaviours.

The birth of a child prompted "Chantelle" to begin changing herself. As a youth, she had been involved in violent crime, often drug-related, and she spent a number of years in youth correctional facilities which she described as a "breeding ground for better criminals." Her training was insufficient to keep her out of prison as an adult. She became a boxer as an outlet for her anger and frustration, and she turned professional following eight successful years at the amateur level. She related well to sports analogies:

> It's one thing to watch it on TV, but it's another thing to actually to be in the ring, take the pain, and deliver and stay focused, and ahh, if you kind of put that in terms of life, a lot of these people have been through some painful past and you know, they're able to take that but also to have some positive energy about and move forward.... (Robertson, 2020 p. 102)

Chantelle credited becoming an athlete with giving her the confidence to become a student, but she credited the birth of her son with her decision to stop criminal activity:

> I think the biggest thing in my life was my son and he is seven now, and I would say that he was kind of like my saviour that when I found out I was pregnant it was.... Suddenly I wasn't just being reckless and just living for myself and I actually, I needed to start caring about something, and he provided that for me, so, like, when he was a baby I wanted to do everything I could to be a good person.... (Robertson, 2020 p. 104)

Although Chantelle lost her son to foster care, she hoped to reunite with him when able to care for him properly. She stopped being a drug user, enrolled in a counselling psychology program at a Canadian university and added "intelligent," "determined," "serious," "responsible," "ex-con," and "counsellor" memes to her self-presentation in Figure 16.

Both Chantelle and Tina (described in Chapter 2) were unable to voice why they would react to their unplanned pregnancies by changing themselves in positive ways, in contrast with other women who maintain dysfunctional lifestyles throughout multiple pregnancies. Both shared a deeply held belief that their parents were deficient in some ways and that they had the ability to be different. From their descriptions, both had been lacking in social interest, and it is plausible that their pregnancies provided them with that interest. By becoming better parents than what they experienced as children, they were committed to making the world a better place for their progeny.

Although Chantelle credited the birth of her son and her career as a boxer as life-changing events that aided her transition, she said there were some constants to her personality that cannot be mapped memetically but were essential to her drive to change. These constants are represented by a bar at the base of her self-map with directional arrows illustrating their importance in animating her being. "Self-changer" is pictured as flowing from empowered animation grounded in spirit, but it was not always present in her self.

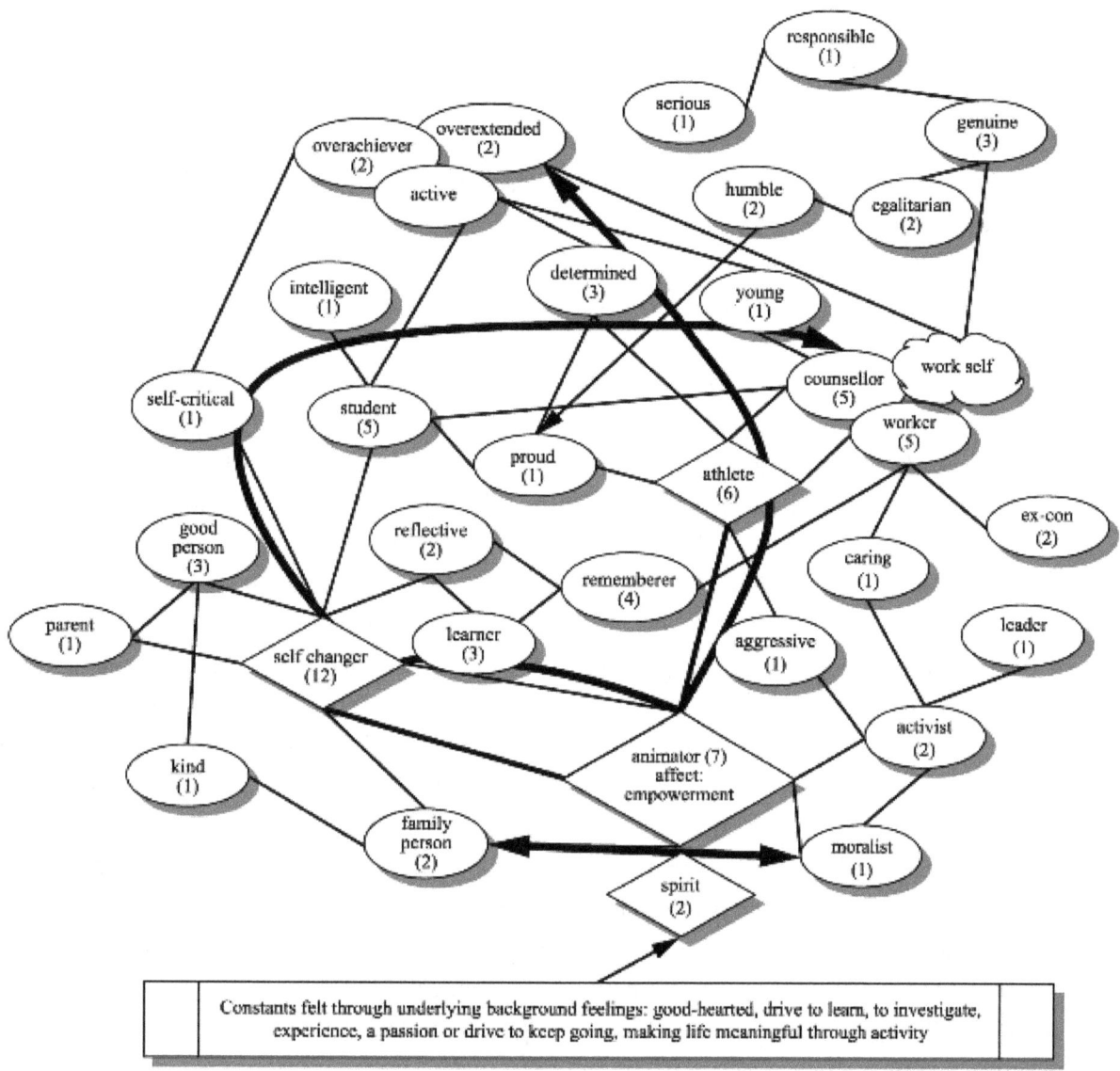

Figure 16: Self-Map of Chantelle – From criminal to counsellor

The decision to change one's life to benefit children is shown by men as well. "Trevor's" self (Robertson, 2020) had a meme for parents, even though he had no biological children at the time of the study. As a child, he was traumatized when abandoned by his father in a northern forest. His role as a protector also stemmed from his family of origin:

> When my dad would drink or when anyone else would drink I would be the protector of the youngest ones, and that sort of shaped my role, sort of shaped how I became a man. (Robertson, 2020 p. 220)

He traced the anger he felt when people abuse children or women to this childhood protector role. While he no longer intimidates people by threatening physical violence, the anger at perceived injustice remains, leading to political activism. His personal quest included developing the ability to feel a full range of emotions and teaching others to become emotionally intelligent.

In these narratives, transitions are pictured as life-transforming events, akin to the religious notion of conversion: A woman gives birth to a baby and becomes a responsible person; a man encounters an insightful and authoritative swimming coach and comes away with sufficient academic self-esteem to enroll in university. If we view the self as an integrated complex structure with individuals presenting different sides of themselves in different contexts, the appearance of sudden change is illusory. The fact that the first two times Tina became pregnant, she modified her behaviour in identical ways suggests that the requisite parenting memes outlining a "pregnancy script" were already in place in her self, waiting to be triggered. Although different presentations triggered by context do not imply self-change, incremental changes to the self are possible. While Brent's transition could be traced to his swimming coach, it was still a matter of years between this intervention and his ultimate enrollment in university. In the meantime, he experimented with coaching others first in one sport (swimming) and then another (cycling). He also experimented by taking responsible positions in his sporting associations and the environmental movement. Each success led to a slight revision of his self that in turn paved the way for further experimentation.

Self-maps are not a neutral technology—they affect the person mapped in some ways. Chantelle reported that seeing her map reminded her to keep to the path she had chosen. Tina decided, between interviews, to become less paranoid and more assertive with her change effort. She decided to refuse to give into her depression, allow her children more freedom to play, and allow her husband to help her with household work. Between interviews, Trevor reframed his "overweight" meme as the less pejorative "big," began engaging in artwork and political activism. Magdelynn said she had become less rigid and less of a role player between interviews, with resultant improved familial and romantic relationships. It appears that the act of seeing one's self-map often allows one to see possibilities without the necessity of having these possibilities suggested by a therapist.

With this self-mapping technique we can recognize conditions that lead to developmental change before any such change occurs. Brent had been shaken by the murder of a fellow cyclist immediately prior to the commencement of this study. He said he felt the deceased person's presence, and he awakened during the night afraid of seeing a ghost. He felt guilty after agreeing with another cyclist that the deceased "could be an asshole sometimes." He began thinking about what people might come to understand of him if he died. While this reflection could result in self-change, none had yet occurred. We might predict, however, that this increased awareness of his own mortality might lead to considerations of his potential legacy and that he would become less aggressive or judgmental in asserting his strongly held beliefs. We might predict increased concerns about family - both with his family of origin and the development of a future family of his own. His self-map appeared to be laying the groundwork for such developments.

The transitions recounted here involved relationships with other people. Those relationships were remembered in narratives that included thematic interpretations of events. The storylines imputed cause and effect. JohnB's relationship with a high school classmate who was non-Christian led to his questioning of church doctrine and eventually to an acceptance of cultural diversity. Trevor (whose self-map is featured in Chapter 7) obtained his Indigenous name in a relationship with an uncle that gave direction to his life. Judy said the criticisms of friends resulted in self-examination and behavioural change. We examined how encouragement Brent received from a swimming instructor eventually led to his teaching career. A friend encouraged Magdelynn to play wheelchair basketball, which eventually led to an invitation to play for the national women's team. Pangloss, whom we touch on in the next section on the False Self, was coached through high school by a paternalistic Sikh who viewed his education to be of paramount importance. Two participants (Tina and Chantelle) experienced lifestyle changes prompted by the birth of children. Since all of these transitional events were based on relationships with other people, we need to consider the implication that therapy cannot be successful without consideration of such relationships and their effect on the self. Some clients, like Olivia and Suzie, had to distance themselves from some relationships to develop and maintain their beneficial transitions. No transitions involved a new self—all were built on an existing one.

If the objective of therapy is change, then self-maps may be thought of as snapshots at a particular point in time. To be effective, the client needs to identify with the snapshot taken with the realization that snapshots taken at different points of time would not be identical. Since the self cannot be viewed as static, it is important to bring into focus the notion of remembered transitions. Once clients can link previous developmental change to who they are in the present, they will be able to better visualize future planned change. Therapists can use the concept of incremental change in planning such developmental transitions.

The False Self and Mini-selves

People may present a false self for fear of retribution. For example, clients whose participation in counselling is a condition for avoiding unwanted consequences with respect to employment or the justice system have an incentive to keep their "real" self hidden. The cost of such a strategy, in addition to the obvious stress of maintaining a deception, is to preclude self-growth. A second possibility is that people who present false selves do so because, like prototypical adolescents, have not yet developed a coherent self-identity. The activity of playing various roles and selves dependent on situation and inclination could become a lifelong habit precluding reflective self-examination. The cost of such a failure to ground oneself is inconsistency with attendant difficulty in establishing and maintaining long-term relationships. A third possible reason for presenting a false self may involve low self-esteem often associated with stigma (Tsang et al., 2023). If an individual suspects self-inadequacy, they may fear confirmation of that inadequacy. The cost of such a strategy is a fragile self with accompanying displays of anger whenever that fragile self is threatened. It is the role of the therapist to identify the reason for false self displays and allay the underlying emotional factors contributing to an unwillingness to engage in self-examination. Clients who present themselves partially or falsely, provided that false presentation persists, will likely get little benefit from the mapping process.

"Pangloss" questioned the accuracy of some information used following the second interview, advising, "I was determined to convince you that there were negatives in my personality, so I presented an inaccurate picture" (Robertson, 2020, p. 143). During his third interview he admitted, "I can exaggerate things to the point of dishonesty." While our remembered narratives will almost always vary from actual events, when those remembrances are experienced as exaggerations, they ring hollow. Although Pangloss was invited to correct his self-map during our third interview, he declined to do so, stating he pays attention to himself only to the extent of its utility, but that he came out of the process of this research as he thought he would: "complicated, contradictory, and confusing." Analysis of his emotional states puts structure on that confusion.

By this third interview, Pangloss decided he wanted the researcher to like him, but with this he expressed a new dilemma. Anything he said to "correct" previous impressions would be reflective of this new emotion with a resultant "feel" of inauthenticity. While admitting he had "faked bad" during the second interview, even the information given in his initial interview was tainted emotionally. Aspects of his self-description as an avenging warrior may have reflected his ideal self as opposed to his real self, but his sexuality, his predilection to action, and his cognitive intellectualizing style were consistent across interviews. His demand for new insights into his self from the researcher was also consistently presented and may have reflected identity confusion resulting from not knowing which "Pangloss" he more closely resembled. With each session we revised his self-map, represented in Figure 17, but no iteration resonated for him. Had he been an actual client, the material shared could have been the basis for more self-exploration and psychological assessment.

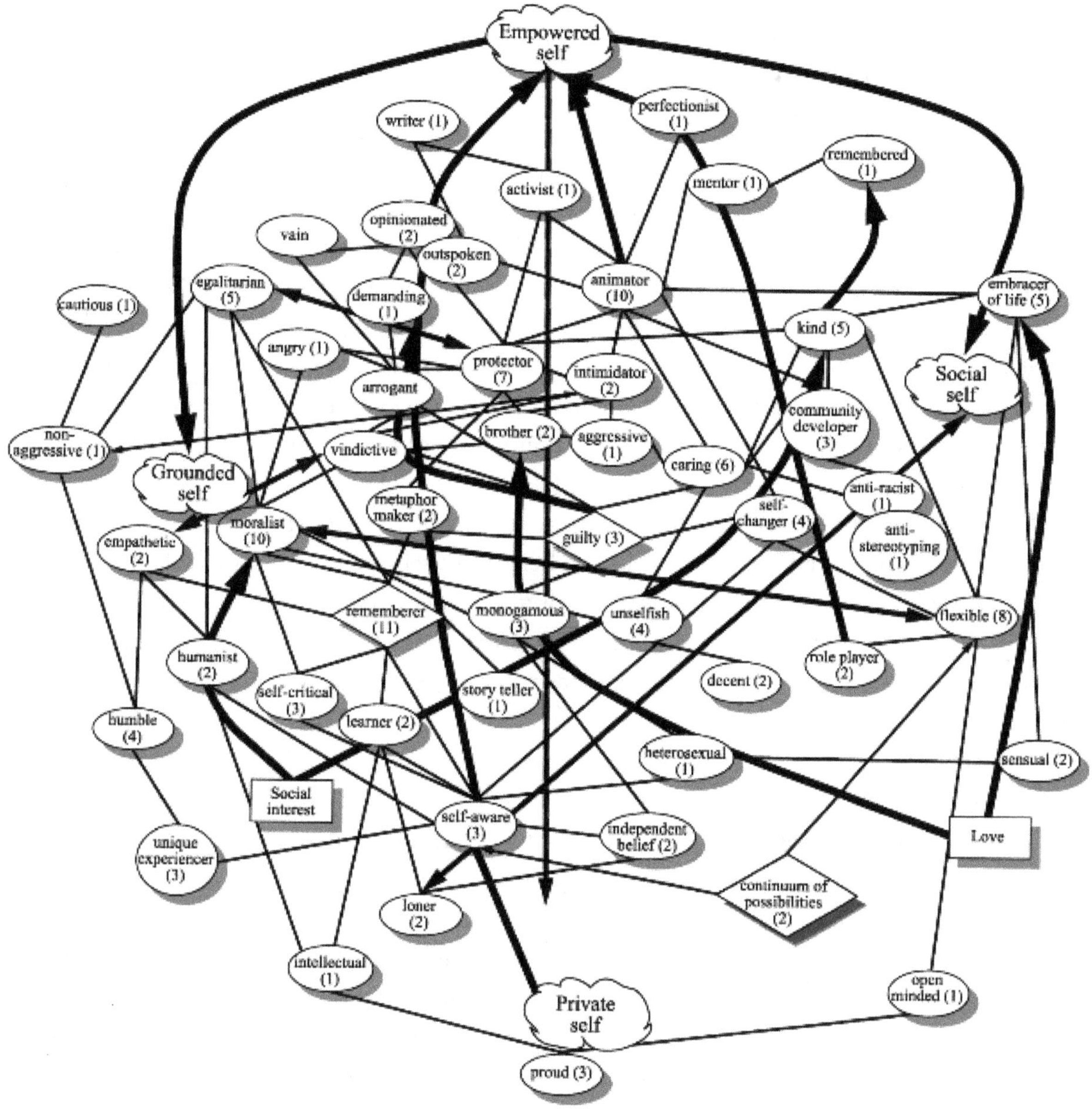

Figure 17: The self of a personified "Judge, Jury and Executioner"

Having to rely, often solely, on the narrative a client provides is at times a struggle in therapy. We are limited by what is shared, what we can see of the person sitting before us, and what we can gather between the things that are said. This challenge continues in the process of self-mapping. Reflecting on why a presentation of a false self may arise provides direction to who may be suitable or unsuitable for the process, and how mapping may be used therapeutically to support those with an incoherent self-identity or those managing low self-esteem to become more grounded in their sense of self.

How do we know when we are facing a false self? While we don't have a complete answer to this question, there are some signs that may indicate the need to consider it a possibility. An analysis of a client's potential benefits and losses to presenting favourably, or unfavourably may support therapists in identifying whether there is a high risk of a false self being presented. If there is a high risk, we should consider the possibility that the client may still be a good candidate for memetic mapping. This may be the case in a court-ordered situation where clients may fear that their true self could get them in more trouble or they are unwilling to fully engage due to it being mandated. Being presented with an incomplete version of the self may happen when sufficient rapport and trust is not yet developed, as occurred with "Tina," who initially withheld being bisexual due to uncertainty about how the researcher would respond. When a client continues to report that he or she does not resonate with the map even after revisions, such as with the example of "Pangloss," there may have been a false or incomplete presentation of self. This is a sign that key components of their present self are missing, or versions of the self are in flux and it is possible the client is not fully ready or willing to look deeper at self-identifying memes. It is fair to expect we will encounter clients unwilling to look at the aspects of themselves they deem more or less desirable, or that attempts to do so may be overwhelming.

To work through the false self, we should ensure we have good rapport with clients, keep in mind their readiness to change, and assess the risks and benefits of self-mapping for each client. Being presented with a false self can be therapeutic by serving to increase self-awareness and internal motivation to change, as long as the client is willing and able to work on it. We must also remember the importance of constancy in the self and reinforce those parts that are adaptive to reduce perceived threat to the perception they have of their self.

As we have seen, memes often form distinct clusters within the self. Often these clusters may represent some aspects of a person's life such as family, striving, empathy, or love. Occasionally we see larger clusters that are not well integrated with the rest of the self. Olivia's initial self (figure 12) had three such clusters labeled "Social Person," "Imperfect," and "Spiritual/Fitness." The Olivia in her "Social Person" self had a different presentation than the depressed person found in her "Imperfect" cluster or her more sanguine spiritual self. With relatively few cognitive pathways between clusters, Olivia tended to stay within each cluster. Therapy consisted, in part, of increasing the memetic pathways between clusters so that she could more easily move between them. These clusters did not present as separate selves—she was still the same person—but her presentation differed dependent on which cluster she happened to inhabit at any given time. We call these larger clusters "mini-selves."

These clusters can be developmental. JohnB traced the developmental evolution of such "mini-selves" (numbered consecutively in Figure 10) beginning with a "Challenger of Authority" theme developed as a youth, which reminds us of Jung's concept of "individuation." He constructed a "Worker/Social" self through conscious role play, and he could invoke either self dependent on context. Finally, using observation, meditation, and social action, he developed a mini-self based on empathy and spirituality. Instead of uniting his self in a coherent whole, it served as an alternate persona to which he could retreat when other "selves" were not needed. He worried that under the layers of self, he did not exist.

"Mini-selves" are not the "false selves" of our previous discussion but are evolved presentations that may be applied in different contexts while nonetheless comprising part of a larger self connected to that self by shared memes. The existence of such mini-selves may challenge the requisite sense of stability and constancy. The challenge of the therapist is to show the internal logic of applying different aspects of self in alternative contexts while finding an underlying constancy that grounds the client.

This sense of constancy may assist clients in overcoming adversity. "Nick" (Robertson, 2020) said his sense of being empowered came from his childhood when he had pneumonia and refused to restrict his physical activity. When sent to Russia from Kazakhstan, he became involved in cross-country skiing and running. As a student, he thought it would be good to see the world, and his academic chair suggested that he go to the US. Although many people had difficulty obtaining visas after the 9/11 terrorist attack, his success led to the belief that if he anticipates something, it will happen. This sense of empowerment reportedly came from inside himself but was re-enforced experientially.

As we can see, mini-selves are often closely tied to key transitions in one's life. Both in the spirit of maintaining a sense of constancy and ensuring an integrated whole, it is important that the mini-selves that are adaptive for the client are well integrated in the core self so they can move in and out of it as needed. At times, maladaptive mini-selves may emerge, as we saw in the case of the suicidal youth discussed in chapter 3. If we look back, we see that the meme "depressed person" was so closely tied to her identity that it became her core. In such cases we need to strengthen adaptive memes or adaptive mini-selves prior to working on weakening the hold of the maladaptive mini-self. Remember it is crucial to maintain a sense of constancy by building upon what is already present and creating an adaptive core so as not to destabilize the sense of self before weakening cores that are no longer serving the person.

A Transsexual Self

Despite identifying as a third gender separate from male or female, she asked to be described by feminine pronouns.[2] She said her self-map (Figure 18) accurately reflected the "war" between two mini-selves: the masculine "Fred" and the feminine "Fredelle." She said that Fredelle embodied all of the things she wanted to be, including being loving, unique, sensual, hopeful and intellectual. Thirty out of 100 segments from her initial two-hour interview were coded for the meme "feminine." The next most coded referent was "transsexual," and it too is found on the Fredelle side of the ledger. The Fred cluster includes mortal, bald, old, self-defeating, and depressed.

The "war" was one-sided, as the empowered animating core is on the feminine side, with the result that any blows directed by her animating centre landed on the passive "Fred." Fred was simply a repository for unwanted characteristics. The perceived antagonism between the feminine and the masculine is further supported by negative or repellent forces between memes for self-defeating (Fred) and nurturing (Fredelle). Fredelle said she wept "tears of joy" as her testicles were removed as part of a series of sex change operations. For Fredelle there could be no accommodation with any part of Fred, who must be eradicated. It was not always thus.

Although there is a biological basis to the self, mini-selves are social constructions. Fredelle recounted a time when she would switch her presentation to Fred dependent on context. She found that demeaning, which is why we see "role player" on the negative side of the ledger.

| 68 | – UNDERSTANDING TRANSITION AND NON-TRANSITION

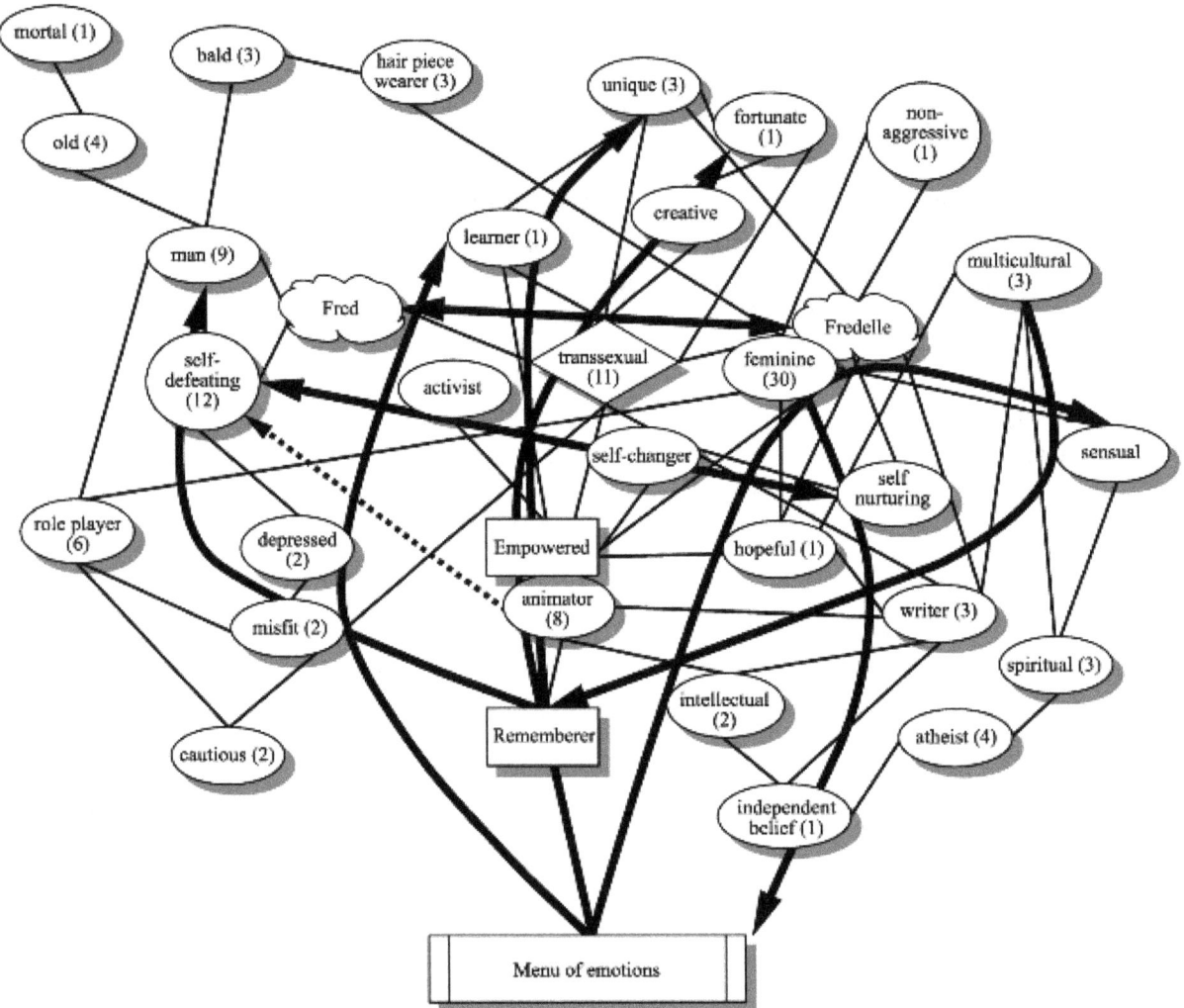

Figure 18: Self-map of "Fredelle" constructed using the narrative method and showing the number of coded segments in brackets and points of internal conflict with double-headed arrows.

The example of Fredelle shows how it is possible for identity to become focused in one mini-self, with the result that it becomes dominant. In point of fact, all negative qualities, including mortal, self-defeating, and depressed, were associated with Fredelle's rejected mini-self, while all positive attributes were associated with the dominant mini-self. In Fredelle's view, there could be no assimilation of qualities that made up her two mini-selves - no resolution to the conflict between the two. Since she had objectively identifiable male characteristics even after sex change surgery, and since she was, in any event, mortal, the "war" could only end in death.

Fredelle described a tormented childhood in which she experimented with her sexual identity only to receive repeated degradation from boys and her father. She recalled, "I was generally treated as someone who was a fag and lower than them and not respected." She was friendless, and she avoided situations of potential ridicule. She recalled:

> I also stuttered very badly; I mean so badly that it was a physical problem. I'd be shaking my head up and down; you would think I was having a seizure if you saw me. I'd be struggling so hard to get that sound out that my jugular veins would be sticking out. I'd be shaking my head; it was a horrible thing. I recall sitting at the supper table trying to talk, and I was sitting against the wall. I'd be banging my head against the wall trying to get a sound out, and I felt like a freak. (Robertson, 2020 pp. 220-21)

Fredelle accepted the label "freak" with the interpretation that being born into a male body was the cause of her freakiness. She became intensely angry with her male side for uncaringly causing so much pain. Fredelle's "coming out" represented self-acceptance. In what has now become a recurrent theme, Fredelle found purpose or social interest in attempting to make the world a better place—in her case through political activism to advance the cause of transsexual persons.

At one level of perception, Fredelle's orchidectomy between our first and second interviews represented radical change; however, when viewed from the perspective of her self, the removal of her testes was a cosmetic change allowing her physical self to conform to her mental reality. In a very post-modernist way, we can become that to which we aspire modifying the evidence provided by our environment to conform to our preferred reality. There is an important caveat on this ability: We are social animals defined by relationships and our ability to force our environment to conform to our preferences is limited by the extent of the changes we can actually engineer and is dependent on the acceptance of our preferred "reality" by significant others. Support for our narrative of reality is a form of legitimization without which our defined self rings hollow. As a child and youth, Fredelle could not construct her own viable narrative, nor was one provided to her that gave her a sense of value or legitimacy. Her political activism may be viewed as an attempt to gain social acceptance for such a narrative, which, in turn, was therapeutic.

Fredelle reported that she was able to feel a range of emotions following the removal of her testes, having associated her former deficit in emotional functioning with maleness. The stereotype of male emotional retardation is readily available within North American culture, but many males do report having a full range of emotions (Robertson, 2018). An alternative explanation in Fredelle's case is that her testes came to represent emotional repression initially required for her own survival (while living as a male), and this led to a failure to develop and substantiate a self-narrative that could give her eudaimonic satisfaction when she began to identify as a woman. She concluded, in her emotional angst, that emotions were not properly part of the self. Her development of a self-enhancing narrative and its acceptance by supportive communities removed the necessity for tight restrictions on her ability to feel emotions. Since the self is an emotional as well as a cognitive structure, the removal of her testes may be seen as a symbolic action that triggered a personal transition toward completeness or wholeness.

Missing from Fredelle's self was identification with community. Before endeavouring to create an active transsexual community in her home city, she found a community of people organized around the Unitarian Church supportive of her transsexual self-definition. She was able to share her identity with these people and receive their acceptance and support. Individuals do not function well, for long, in splendid isolation. We need the affirmation of people around us to maintain our identities. This requires some flexibility, as all relationships involve negotiation.

Revising client self-maps

Once our initial interpretation of the self-map is completed, we can collaboratively work to modify the maps so that it better represents the client, or we can examine ways the self that is represented can change. There are numerous possible directions and how this is accomplished is dependent on the process co-constructed with the client. Here are some ways we can begin:

1. Identify core elements that are missing or dysfunctional. Explore with the client whether these missing elements are truly not part of their self or whether they were simply missed in the initial interview.
2. Bring forth client awareness of unconscious or unacknowledged characteristics they possess. This may be a time to use immediacy in sharing what we see within the client.
3. Support clients in increasing their awareness of unconsciously held worldviews. Explore triggers to unhelpful behaviours and the evidence that supports a currently held dysfunctional worldview contributing to unhelpful behaviour.
4. Identify central themes and clusters to support the client in understanding the behavioural patterns and their triggers.
5. Identify a menu of emotions that are common to the client and notice what parts of the self each emotion triggers. These are the long-range connections.
6. Identify parts of the self the client wishes to change. Have the client come up with gradual changes they can make to support this change, providing ideas where needed.
7. Listen for possible reframes for those memes clients would like to change. For instance, Tina reframed "oversensitive" to "sensitive," which was no longer seen as a negative.
8. Support those parts of the self already present that support the desired change. This is part of ensuring there is a sense of constancy despite making changes.
9. Develop a behavioural plan to implement desired change while being true to oneself.

In the process of enacting change, we must keep in mind client limitations and do our best to adjust to where the client is at. As you have likely noticed, some of the maps, more than others, became quite complex. It is not uncommon for me (TJR) to have clients initially feel somewhat overwhelmed as they look at their map. It is helpful to slow it down by gathering their impressions and having them voice what they are noticing. I also share the map each time we make changes so they can see it coming together. Sometimes the overwhelm is facing what they perceive as the darker parts of themselves they try to ignore; other times it's observing the interconnectedness of memes. Their responses help to inform what their capacity is for self-understanding and chang, remembering it is a collaborative process.

As the mapping process can be quite abstract and varies from person to person, we have tried to make clear how the process can be done with the use of steps to outline stages. While the steps to prepare the maps are established, there is no clearly defined way to use mapping to effect change. While we offer some ideas and ways it can be used to enact change these are not hard and fast rules and your own therapeutic style should be incorporated. Fortunately, the process of creating self-maps often results in client-generated change.

---

[1] The stories of Judy, Magdelynn and JohnB are detailed in The Evolved Self (2020)

[2] Fredelle used the term "transsexual" to describe who she was. Her use of this term recognized two biological sexes with the implication that one can transition between the two with sex change operations. Sometimes the term "transgender" is used as a synonym for "transsexual" but that would be inappropriate her. The term "gender" was appropriated from the study of grammar in 1955 by psychologist John Money to refer to culturally learned sex roles – male and female. Using a more fluid definition of "gender," Fredelle declared that she represented a third gender that was neither male nor female. She chose female pronouns because of her antipathy for her male side; however, had "gender neutral" pronouns such as "Ze" or "Xe" been common at the time she may have claimed the use of one of them instead of the term "she."

7

Working with Clients from Collectivist Cultures

Minority clients have responded to culturally responsive counsellors with increased willingness to return to counselling, more expressed satisfaction, and greater depth of disclosure (Ponterotto, Fuertes, & Chen, 2000; Hinton & Kirmayer, 2016). Cultural norms may vary with respect to defining behavioural strengths, benchmarks establishing counsellor or helper credibility, and preferences with respect to possible interventions. The ability to perceive possible areas of cultural difference and to respond flexibly and positively to such differences is crucial when working with clients from disparate cultural groups (Robertson et al., 2015). Cultures may be viewed as a series of probabilities based on the frequency of defining memes in a given population. Since no one individual will match perfectly a given cultural stereotype, the proficient counsellor will be open to exploring internal cultural variation within all clients. At its core, proficient multicultural counselling is simply good counselling practice that recognizes individual difference.

Counselling and therapy, predicated on respecting the uniqueness of the individual, avoids many of the pitfalls attributed to ethnocentric practice. By learning the client's worldview, the counsellor comes to understand those genetic, cultural, and environmental factors, and the interpretations thereof, that shape the client's self. Each person may be understood as having an internal culture of one. Mapping the self helps us develop an understanding and appreciation of that internal culture. Armed with such knowledge, the counsellor is better able to identify those behavioural strengths, values, and practices that uniquely make up the individual. With such an approach, it is possible to effectively engage in therapeutic change while having little previous experience with the client's culture.

While we are entering a discussion of collectivist cultures and how self-mapping applies, it is worth noting our discussion centers around cultures that are aboriginal to Canada. With roots from northern Saskatchewan, both authors work predominantly with aboriginal clients. The lead author was president and elected director of his local Indian and Metis Friendship Centre for 14 years, and his work history includes having been Director of Health and Social Development for the Federations of Saskatchewan Indian Nations, Lifeskills Coordinator with the Saskatchewan Indian Federated College (now First Nations University), and as Director of Training and Program Development for Indian Child and Family Services, La Ronge, Saskatchewan. The information we share is grounded in research but also involves perspectives learned from living and working in aboriginal communities and the variations in worldview and memes within that we have lived and witnessed.

Following this discussion, we briefly explore a map developed with someone from the interior of China and flow into examining some of the effects of religion on the self.

Working with the Indigenous Self

It may surprise the reader that Tina, whose self-map was presented in Chapter 4, is an aboriginal woman who lived her entire life in an isolated northern community where people engage in a traditional lifestyle of hunting, fishing, and trapping. Yet, there are no identifiable markers of aboriginality on her self-map. Tina's concerns were with family, children, and work. Her social activism included advocating for students at school and promoting acceptance of lesbian and bisexual people. When asked, she would admit to being Metis, a people recognized as aboriginal in Canada by the Constitution Act of 1982, but this was not how she defined her self. She was a wife, mother, activist, learner, and decent person first and foremost who happened to have Metis ancestry.

"Trevor" came from a different direction in life. He was born and raised in a southern city by alcoholic parents who did not live a traditional lifestyle. In contrast with Tina, Trevor decided as a young man that he needed markers of aboriginality in his self; but to accomplish this he needed to feel that these markers were true. He took steps to establish his aboriginal identity, reproduced in figure 19.

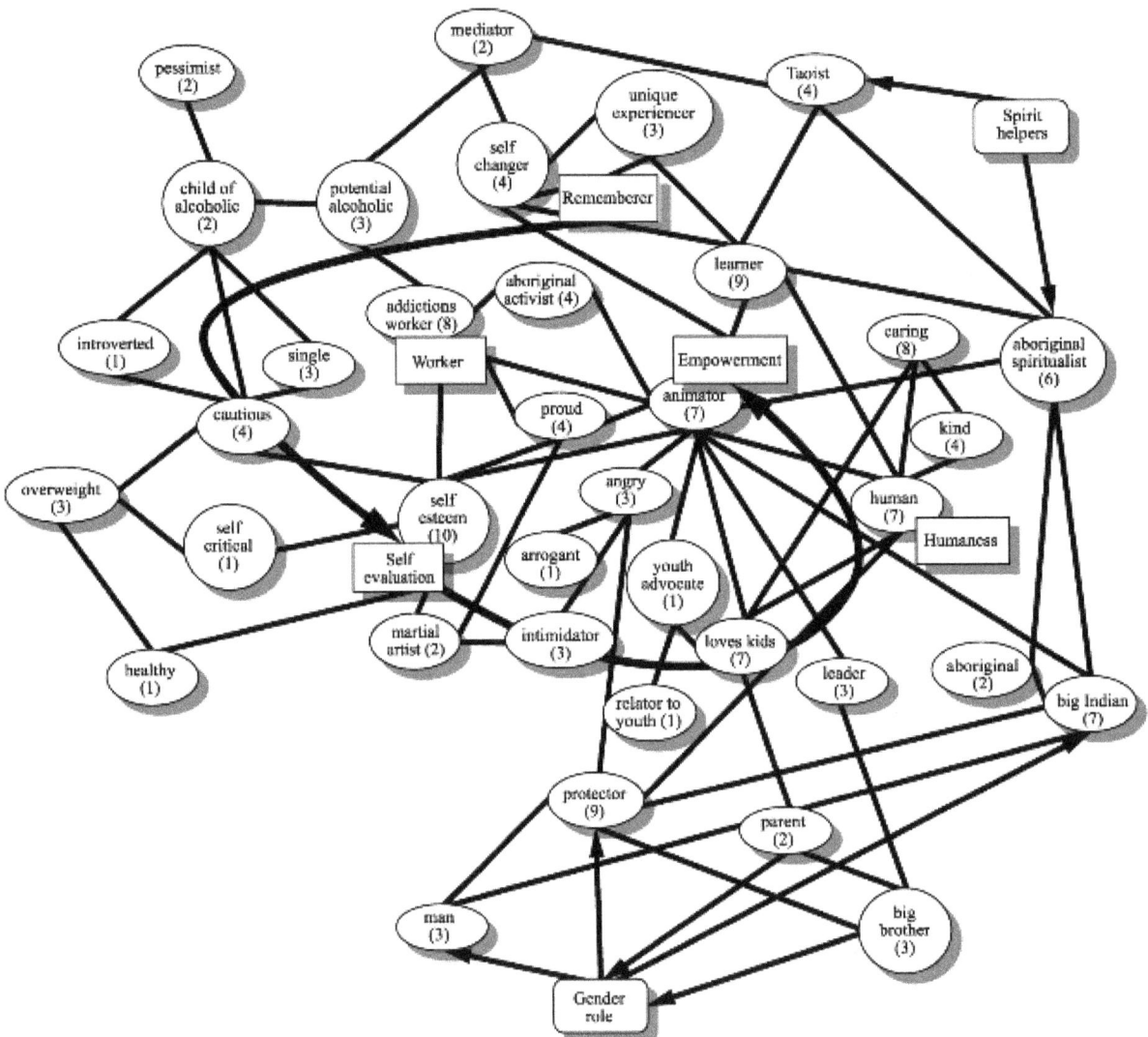

Figure 19: Initial self-map of a young Cree man seeking to define his aboriginality

Trevor effectively had to raise his younger siblings because their parents were often absent. Criminal gangs were active in the part of the city in which he lived, so he had to be tough. He befriended and took training from a martial arts instructor. He reported anger issues. He once smashed a window of a late-model car when the occupant propositioned a female friend on the street, even though that was her profession. Another time he threatened a man in a mall after he witnessed him hitting his child. His motto at the time was, "Nobody messes with a big Indian."

> So then I thought, 'What's it mean to be Indian?' And I thought, 'warrior,' so I did some research, and I realized back in the old days we used to go on vision quests, so I went on a vision quest. (Robertson 2020, p. 120)

With the guidance of a traditional elder[1], Trevor became a drum keeper and a powwow singer, and he named the Taoism he learned from his martial arts instructor along with aboriginal spirituality as his spirit helpers. Note that both spirit helpers appear on the periphery of Trevor's self-map. The core of his self developed before he encountered either.

The self may be viewed as a product of the narratives we tell ourselves about ourselves, with memes providing an outline. The thick black circular line in figure 19 forms the outline of the initial story Trevor gave the counsellor at their first session when he was asked to describe who he was. He had begun by talking about how he had the ability to change and that he had begun life as a child of alcoholics and was, therefore, a potential alcoholic. He talked about being introverted and cautious as a child with low self-esteem. He admitted his response had been to become an intimidator and admitted, "I can still be an asshole at times." Through it all he had come to appreciate himself as a human who gets things done. The last quality was coded for "animator" as part of the theme "Empowerment."

The self-map in figure 19 was presented to Trevor at his second session. He paused with his mouth half open and said, "It's almost prophetic... I would not have called myself an aboriginal activist when I first met you, but I do now and here it is in my map!" It was explained that there was nothing prophetic here, that segments in his story or narrative involving his attempts to expose doctors who overprescribe medicines to aboriginal people and attempts to get street prostitutes to change their lifestyles were coded as aboriginal activism. This was consistent with his empowered animator self and the idealism he had shown as an addictions worker. Excited, Trevor explained that his activism had matured and that he was now involved in his band's politics and lobbying elected governments for needed services. He explained, "It was like igniting a fire that keeps me focused on something bigger than myself."

Trevor's activism inspired him to write poetry and songs critical of society and greed. It seemed that "Rememberer," "activist," "empowerment/animator," and "caring" had converged to create a new meme, "artist," within Trevor's self. Directional arrows from those initiating centres were added to his revised self-map showing this relationship. He intentionally replaced the overweight meme with the less pejorative "big." The meme "single" was changed to "dating." Recognizing that using his size, martial arts training, and arrogance to intimidate others was a denial of their humanity and his own, he decided to modify this behaviour, in part, by sublimating his aggressiveness into political activism. Figure 20 incorporates these changes and those of a subsequent interview.

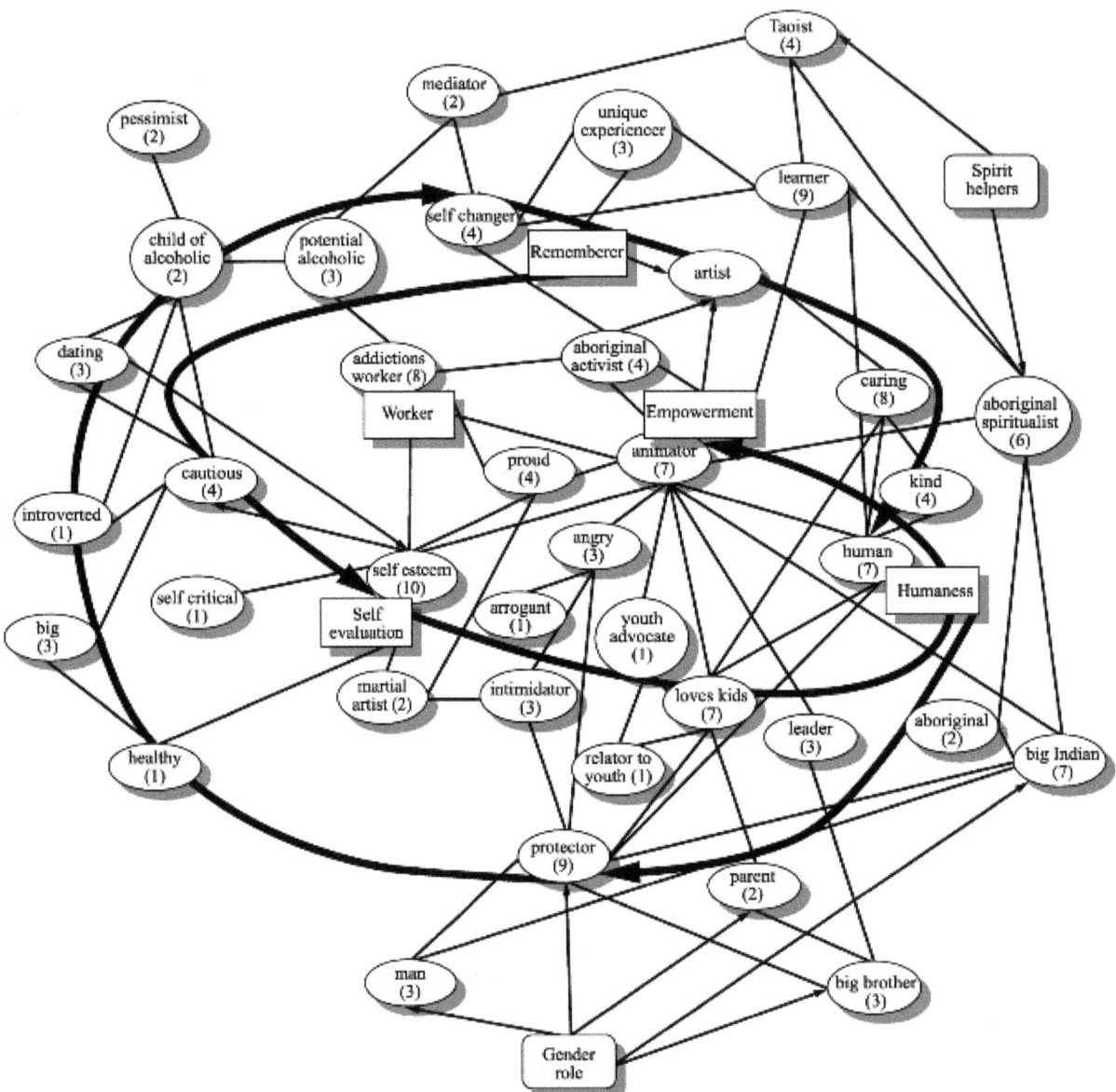

Figure 20: Final revised self-map of the young Cree man "Trevor."

During our final meeting, Trevor said that there was a second self-defining narrative in the map that ran in the opposite direction to the first. He said that he had been reflecting on what the theme "Humanness" meant and he concluded that it referred to thinking and feeling with an emphasis on compassion. He said his interest in aboriginality was a subset of this humanness and that his role as a "parent" and "protector" was a subset of that. He said his protector role and his introversion had affected his dating and that needed to change because it is not healthy. All that could be understood as the product of being from a dysfunctional alcoholic home, but he was capable of change as he proved by developing his artistic side by being more caring and kind to himself. This narrative is outlined by a second thick black arrow running clockwise through his self.

Returning to the theme of dating, Trevor reflected on why his relationships had never lasted in the past. He concluded that as a protector and saviour, he was attracting needy people intent on using him as a co-dependent. He decided he needed to find a strong partner that could support his social activism.

Trevor was a research participant and his changes were self-directed as a result of his participation in the self-mapping exercise. They did not result from direct intervention on the part of the psychologist. As with Tina, seeing himself graphically encouraged reflection which, in turn, generated therapeutic possibilities. This has also been our experience with traditional clients, as with the example of Olivia discussed earlier.

The examples of Tina, Trevor, and others (Robertson, 2014a) demonstrate that there is no aboriginal self per se, that people who have ancestry aboriginal to any given place in the Americas (or elsewhere) can exhibit a spectrum of highly individualized selves. This has implications for cross-cultural counselling. Korhonen (2002) used grounded theory to compare the counselling practices of Inuit people with those offering Western schools of psychotherapy. She was surprised to find fundamental commonalities between modern counselling theories such as CBT, narrative therapy and humanistic schools of psychology. She expressed greater surprise at finding commonalities between those theories and the practices of traditional aboriginal elders engaged in counselling. Western theorists and Inuit elders alike believed in the interrelatedness of emotion, thought, and behaviour, and in the inseparability of the client from his social context. The individual was recognized as the locus of counselling change, with the intention for self-change formed within a unique worldview that includes context-specific goals and predictions of consequence. The fact that the Inuit were effectively the last aboriginal people on the American continents to be colonized lends significance to these findings. Some of the elders in Korhonen's study would have been children when first contact was made with people of European descent.

If fundamental cross-cultural commonalities to counselling practice exist, what can be said of cultural difference? Noting that aboriginal and international students often do not use university counselling services, the lead author designed his doctoral practicum to offer alternative services in settings amenable to the targeted client populations: the university's Native and International Student centres. Aboriginal students did not typically book appointments through the receptionist. Instead, they would "hang around" until the counsellor's door was open and then politely introduce themselves, often engaging in idle chat, presenting an issue, and making an appointment after they felt comfortable with the relationship. Often, they came with complete narratives that needed voice, with the result that the "50-minute hour" became inoperative. Often, they were concerned with integrating the counselling practices with existent belief systems that were held to be traditional. Occasionally the client did not feel comfortable in an office setting, and counselling would take place outside under the trees. The service was effective in broadening counselling services to underserved populations, and the university found funding to continue this specialized position in future years.

The Inuit elders in Korhonen's study viewed counselling as non-directive, and it is precisely this non-directiveness that allows counselling to be multicultural. But traditional elders commonly do more than counsel, and in some roles may be quite directive. They may be herbalists, shamans, and keepers of religiously held supernatural belief systems. In defining the role of counsellor or therapist, individuals from collectivist societies may use analogues such as elder in a directive role, thus miscasting the professional as an expert advice giver. Just as additional time may be required to learn the personal culture of the client, it may be necessary to spend additional time in cross-cultural situations explaining and negotiating the role of the counsellor. While that role may be non-directive, as a diagnostician, the psychologist often assumes an expert stance, and in such cases, diagnoses should be made carefully. For example, a diagnosis of a verbal learning disability might be inappropriate in an individual who is culturally predisposed to place greater value on nonverbal skills. A diagnosis of attention deficit hyperactivity disorder might be inappropriate for an individual from a society where hyper-vigilance is required.

After reviewing nine studies showing low rates of diagnosed post-traumatic stress disorder in U.S. Amerindian populations, Waldram (2004) argued, "It is crucial to consider that aboriginal peoples may exhibit low rates of diagnosed PTSD because they have low rates of PTSD" (p. 221). Since humans share a similar biological platform, it is intuitive to think Waldram must be wrong: Potentially trauma-producing incidents should produce similar rates of PTSD in divergent populations. It is possible that PTSD in aboriginal people was underdiagnosed due to a failure to recognize culturally mediated symptoms. Working in British Columbia, Canada, Brasfield (2001) noted symptoms among some former students of Indian residential schools, that varied from PTSD in some ways. While sleep disturbance, difficulties concentrating, anxiety reactions to triggering stimuli, and the emotional re-experiencing of past events were commonly expressed, these students also displayed extreme and irrational anger, aversion to aboriginal cultures, attachment difficulties, and a propensity toward drug abuse. This symptom complex was not restricted to students who had suffered physical and sexual abuse but included those who had no recollection of an initiating traumatic event. Further, their descendants also displayed the symptomatology. Brasfield argued this collection of symptoms was a form of PTSD, which he labelled Residential School Syndrome (RSS); however, aspects of its etiology, such as the absence of a life-threatening triggering event, aversion to symbols not representative of the stimulus, and the heritability of the condition, indicate RSS is a separate condition dependent on the historical and cultural contexts in which it arose (Robertson, 2006). A discussion of those conditions is necessary to understand their possible effect.

During the final quarter of the nineteenth century, the government of Canada contracted three Christian churches to provide residential education to aboriginal children and youth. While initially only three such schools were planned to service all of western Canada, in practice churches would build a school and demand funding for construction costs retroactively, and by 1931 eighty such schools were in existence. The churches' plan to pay for the maintenance of these schools through student labour using an industrial school model, failed to generate anticipated revenue. Resultant cutbacks in nutrition and health care contributed to high mortality rates. After 1920, student attendance at school became mandatory and truant officers or police acting as truant officers enforced attendance. Many students faced physical and sexual abuse. Such experiences could trigger PTSD, but the existence of additional non-PTSD symptoms and the existence of PTSD-like symptoms in the absence of a triggering incident require explanation. The theory of self used to create maps in this manual provides such an explanation.

Indian residential schools were developed to effect a mass change on a culture. Often children were not allowed to speak their native languages and daily religious instruction, during which traditional aboriginal beliefs were characterized as heathen, was compulsory. Sexuality was often repressed. With missionary zeal, the churches were attempting to replace aboriginal worldviews, and they had a captive audience relatively free from family or community influence with which to work. The churches did not have the knowledge to take into account the aboriginal memes already within the selves of the children, nor did they understand how their new Eurocentric memes would interact with those already in place. Further, they offered a simplified caricature of a Euro-Canadian self from which these children could model. Given these conditions, we would expect many of the residential school students to develop structurally incomplete and conflicted selves even in the absence of overt sexual and physical abuse. Since the self both creates and is created by the surrounding culture, the self-structure and associated worldviews that emerged from this educational process would subsequently be transmitted intergenerationally by ordinary cultural mechanisms. If complete sequences of healthy memes are typically unavailable in the local culture, then unhealthy selves become normative. In such circumstances, individual treatment or psychotherapy is less efficient than community development.

The experience of one northern community illustrates the tie between cultural history and community mental health (see: Robertson, 2015). Stanley Mission is a Cree-speaking community established by Anglican missionaries in 1851, but by the 1990s, four to twelve suicide attempts were occurring in this community of 1,100 every month. The majority of suicide attempts were by youth aged 14 to 25. In 1994, following the death of a 12-year-old girl, one of the authors (LHR) was invited to conduct a post-traumatic stress debriefing with clinic health staff. Community members came to the clinic visibly grieving, and they were invited to join the debriefing. A "talking circle" format allowed everyone in attendance to speak their thoughts and feelings with group support. Community members kept arriving and the meeting had to be moved to a larger location. Grief turned into action. The community held a series of bereavement workshops, developed a volunteer crisis intervention team, and organized group counselling for people experiencing anger, depression, and self-esteem issues. Informal leaders organized a referendum banning alcohol from the community and worked with police to enforce that ban. They built a youth activity centre and equipped it with donations. They implemented workshops on sexual abuse prevention in both elementary and high schools. They organized elders to teach youth survival skills in the boreal forest. They agreed to store all firearms in lockers built for that purpose at a local cooperatively owned store. Parental patrols enforced a 10:00 P.M. curfew for all children under the age of 16. They did not have another completed suicide for a period of six years. But during that interval, divisions surfaced.

The band's health department, headquartered in another community 80 kilometres distant, threatened the community's elder support worker with disciplinary action for not sufficiently promoting Aboriginal Spirituality[2]. The community elders said they recognized that historically their people had not always been Anglican, but their ancestors had voluntarily settled at the mission generations earlier. They also noted that many of the forms of aboriginal spirituality being promoted had never been part of the northern Woodland Cree traditions.

The modern self described here is several thousand years old and combines elements of both individualism and collectivism. The basic structure is cross-cultural. The selves of all cultures exhibit a capacity for volition, uniqueness, continuity, productivity, intimacy, social interest, and reflectivity. The elders in this community were Anglican and were satisfied that their selves and worldviews were healthy and meaningful. A major problem the community faced in the 1990s and prior had been insufficient transmission of those worldviews to younger generations. The community development initiative also re-established the community's volitional will to solve its own problems. The arrival of a new essentialist program questioning the elders' worldview disrupted their transmission of values and weakened the will of informal leaders in the community development enterprise. The local steering committee leading the community development effort stopped meeting. Increasing numbers of community members returned to being the recipients of services instead of actors solving their own problems. Alcohol and drug abuse became widespread again, and predictably, the community suffered a relapse in youth suicidality.

While it is important for those cross-cultural counsellors and therapists working with aboriginal people to have an understanding of the attending historical and socio-economic issues, the lessons presented here are universal. There are probably people in every culture who carry with them a template on how people within that culture should be, and there are just as likely people, and communities of people, in those very same cultures who defy those templates. It is not the business of the therapist to enforce a particular collectivist model on their clients.

In an essentialist view, people of aboriginal descent without sufficient markers of aboriginality in their presentation might be deemed to be unhealthy. Therapists operating from such assumptions might destabilize people like Tina, who did not contain markers of aboriginality. In the end, it is the task of everyone to create self-centric worldviews with all the information available. This is more difficult for a colonized people, at least during the early stages of colonization, because the old worldviews are no longer operative. From this perspective, the term "Historic Trauma" (Wesley-Esquimaux & Smolewski, 2004) might be understood as an idiomatic *sociological* metaphor for the cultural stress that comes with forced change. After decades of work with aboriginal inmates in Canada's penitentiaries, Waldram (2014) was not sure whether this idiom was reducing distress or creating it. A process of indigenization connects modern concepts with traditional aboriginal values thus avoiding a reified view of culture that discounts naturalistic and scientific approaches (Robertson, 2021).

We hold that cultures are fluid concepts that consist of generally shared experiences or generic representations that may be called cultural schemas (Quinn, 2011). By taking the view that all cultures are "aggregates evolved from historical and contemporary appropriation, then each participant in the cultural project becomes an authorized speaker capable of investing in culture in creative ways with applications dependent on context and purpose" (Robertson, et. al., 2020, pp. 17-18).

Individuals within any given culture may have rigid ideas about cultural norms and the people who fail to meet these norms. For example, a client may hold that a particular medicine wheel representing physical, mental, spiritual and emotional quadrants is official or "true," and that aboriginal people who do not share this belief have "lost" their culture in some ways. The lead author has shown how this particular medicine wheel is not traditional and that other medicine wheels illustrating holism are possible (Robertson, 2021). None-the-less, it would be unethical for a counsellor to attempt to change the belief of a client on this or any other matter unless 1) the belief were leading to psychological difficulty and 2) the client agreed to examine possibilities for change. We hold that ethically counselling and psychotherapy must be client-directed. The expertise of the counsellor is on how people can change but the decision to change must come from the client.

While the use of a reified Medicine Wheel both constrains the presentation of the self and externalizes the direction of change, the medicine wheel concept is both in keeping with aboriginal tradition and consistent with a non-directive view of counselling. Counsellors may use the concept of the medicine wheel without teaching any one form as correct. The lead author used this principle while teaching a university class on aboriginal medicines. Students were invited to each create a personal medicine wheel illustrating the aspects of themselves contributing to the whole. The number of categories students divided their personal medicine wheels into varied from three to 18.

The medicine wheel concept may be used to examine, holistically, the practise of counselling and psychotherapy. Figure 21 recognizes a continuum between physical and mental states on the x axis and active and passive states on the y axis.

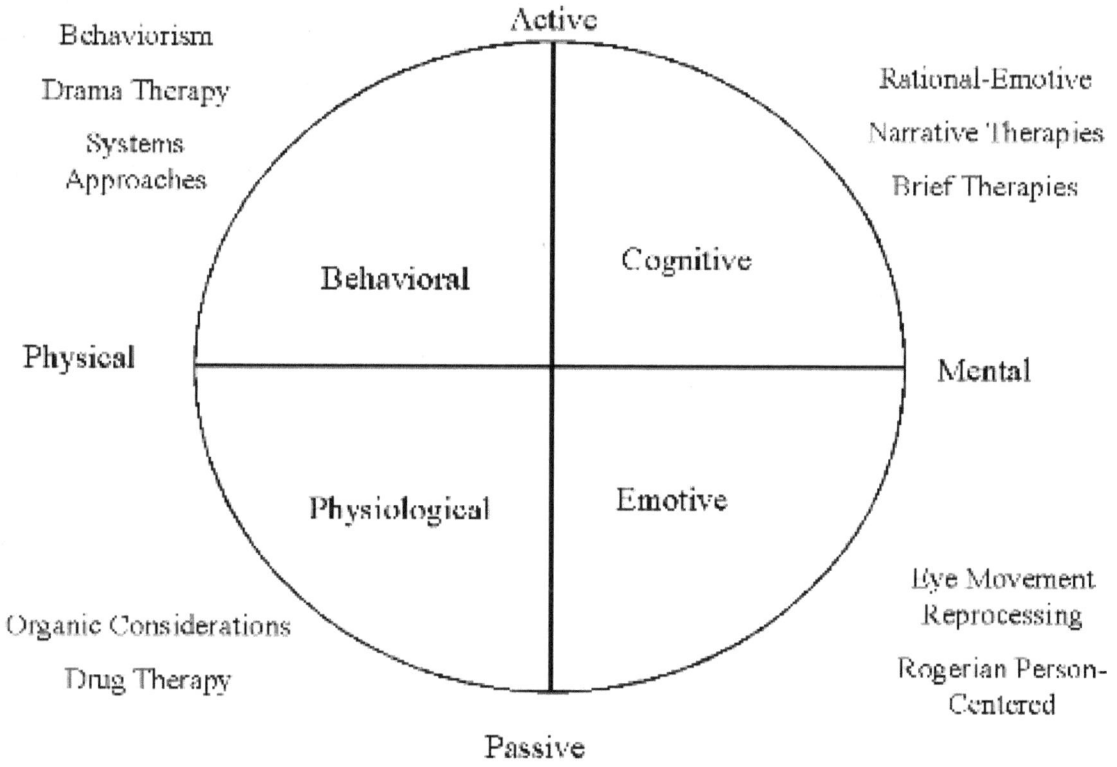

Figure 21: An application of the aboriginal concept of the medicine wheel to the practise of counselling psychology situating various therapies in quadrants defined by two axes: physical/mental and active/passive.

The intersection of the two axes creates four quadrants labelled: cognitive, emotive, physiological and behavioural. Various therapies were situated on those quadrants based on their primary focus.

Given a holistic perspective, it is anticipated that intervention directed at any one quadrant will necessarily create change in the other three. Thus, a client with Attention Deficit Disorder could be given stimulant medication with the expected result that the medication will influence subsequent emotions, cognitions and behaviour. Similarly, a behavioural plan directed at the same condition would be expected to produce changes in the client's cognitions, emotional functioning and physiology.

The Appeal of Collectivism

Maomao, whose map is illustrated in figure 22, attempted to engage the individualism and volitional will inherent in her self, but in the end she concluded this was "too much work," and she opted to be, in her words, "a robot" and wait for the commands mandated by the collectivist society of her origin. She had received a traditional upbringing in the interior of China. She was an only child, and she attributed the expectation that she obey to that status. Decisions ranging from what classes she would take at university to what clothes she would wear on a daily basis were made by her parents. She described herself as a "robot always waiting for the command." She was not totally robot-like. When she attended university in Beijing, she bought a small dog without her parents' permission, which she named "Maomao." She left little Maomao in her parent's care when she was accepted into a doctoral program in Canada. After the dog died, she gave herself the pseudonym for the purposes of this study.

Maomao's self-map has the seven components of the self named earlier; however, memes implying personal volition are found close to the periphery. The core of Maomao's self is deference, family person, and daughter, with obedience to authority being connotatively and behaviourally implied in all three. She had an emotional crisis on arriving in Canada because she did not have a telephone connection with her family for three days. She joined a fundamentalist Chinese Christian church and received direction from that source. She reported, however, that when she received direction that she did not like, she would feel sad and angry.

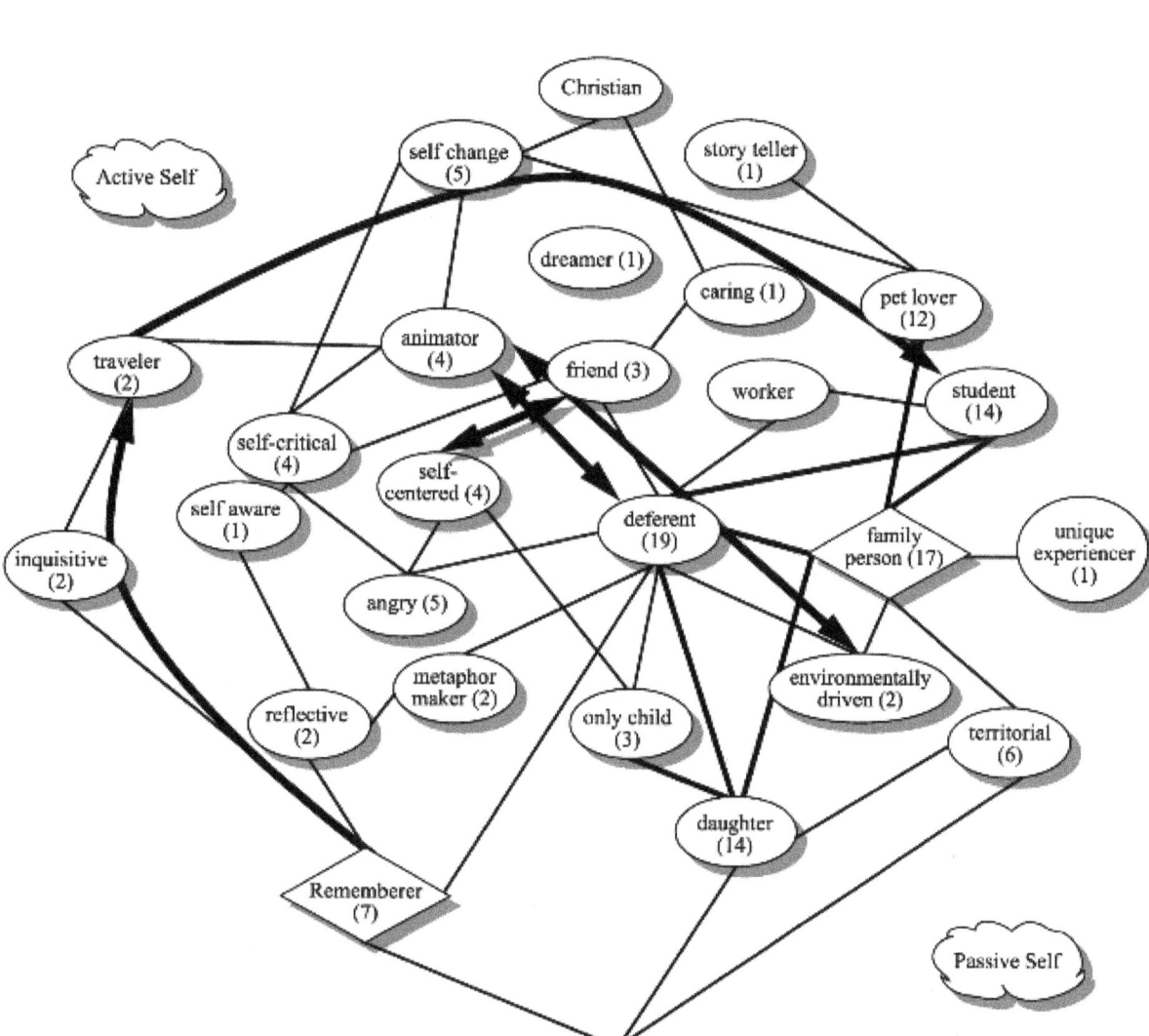

Figure 22:: The self-map of a woman from a collectivist culture with a repressed volitional self.

Maomao had felt sad and angry when she was informed that she would not be majoring in astronomy in Beijing because her parents had decided that computer science was a better field. She excelled in her master's program and was accepted into a doctoral program at a Canadian university.

Maomao reported that when she experienced panic on her arrival in Canada because she was initially unable to connect with her parents by telephone. She became part of a Chinese Christian church and reported that the pastor was very helpful in advising her on how to live. Even her doctoral dissertation was not of her choosing – it was suggested by her dissertation supervisor. After seeing her initial self-map, she decided to enroll in an astronomy class in Canada.

She decided that to make good decisions, she would need to predict possible outcomes using a cost/benefit analysis. She applied this rule for all decisions, including mundane tasks such as what to eat for breakfast and what to wear for the day. After three months of independent decision making she decided it was too much work and that she would go back to being a "robot" because then she would have the time to do things that she enjoyed.

"Individualist" westerners overwhelmingly follow habit, significant others, peers, authorities, and advertisers applying the kind of rational thinking used by Maomao in special or unusual circumstances. Ironically, Maomao had to use her volitional centre to reach the decision to not be volitional. Once she decides to "wait for the command, she needs to rank order those authorities she will obey in case of disagreement between them. In any case, her volitional centre remains available, ready to be activated on her command.

While Maomao represents a sample of one and should not be generalized as applying to other people from collectivist cultures, her example illustrates the ways people from collectivist cultures may experience individualist societies on arrival. Non-directive client-centred therapists will respect her decision to forgo volitional will. We can assist these clients by helping them anticipate and solve problems that will inevitably arise irrespective of whether they choose a more collectivist or a more individualist orientation. For example, had Maomao chosen to stay with a more individualist orientation, she would have potentially alienated people in her collectivist support group. Choosing to engage with a Christian church could have potentially alienated her parents who were not Christian. While therapy is about self-change, counselling is more about problem solving and planning.

Religion and popular culture

Religions serve to position people into permissible roles based on status and attributed characteristics thereby governing acceptable relationships within a given society. Given that we interpret ourselves into existence as a product of such relationships, it would be reasonable to assume that we are largely defined by dominant religions even where the individual is not religious. For example, we saw how Pangloss viewed some people as intrinsically evil and deserving of punishment. There is a similar meme in the Judeo-Christian tradition, and even had he not been raised Christian, Pangloss would have still encountered that meme in the popular culture.

Counsellors and therapists who make assumptions about the optimal religious or spiritual presentation of clients based on ethnic or racial preconceptions may be unwittingly acting as agents of oppression. Changes in religious belief may be developmentally transitional, even in clients who continue to maintain the religious label given to them in childhood. While the counsellor can benefit from understanding the family, community, and societal contexts within which the client is embedded so as to assist the client in making informed decisions, the counsellor cannot constrain those decisions based on such background knowledge.

In this counselling model, the mantle of expertise with respect to culture and self-knowledge passes to the client. With this orientation it is possible to construct a cognitive map of the self and plan developmental or therapeutic change without intimate knowledge of the client's culture. While such knowledge may be an asset in some respects, that very knowledge may lead to inaccurate generalizations and assumptions regarding the identity and worldview of the individual as an individual. The self is never static, it is always in a state of becoming.

It is not possible for the counsellor to become expert with respect to every representative group in a multicultural society. The role of the counselling psychologist is to assist the client in making their implicit theory of self explicit with added insight into the direction of change. Once voiced, the client takes agentive control over the very formulation that allows that control. The combination of the structural qualities of self - distinctness, continuity, individuality, community, even agency itself - becomes his or her own. Emphasis is placed on the understanding of meaning from the client's point of view, with attention paid to how group membership is negotiated and maintained.

The concept of the meme allows for consideration of individual differences and unique linkages. We are simultaneously cultural beings, and in the therapeutic relationship the counsellor explores the individually held culture of the client. As an example, one of the previous clients of LHR was a Zoroastrian client from a Middle Eastern country. The counsellor's previous knowledge of the religion was limited to a historical notation that the Judeo-Christian notion of Satan is descended from the ancient Zoroastrian god Ahriman.

The Zoroastrian client was in his thirties and presented with an inability to form meaningful relationships with women. Since age 17, whenever he had noticed an attractive young woman, he would experience subsequent vivid misogynous dreams involving beating, torturing, and murder. He rarely ejaculated as a result of these dreams but reported a sense of satisfaction associated with the woman's pain while in his dream state. In an attempt to minimize the recurrence of such horrendous nightmares, he had avoided relationships for almost two decades.

The client did not recall any instances of abuse during his upbringing, and he had not felt terrorized by the religious majority in his country of origin. Sex before marriage was a religious taboo, and he had not been allowed to have girlfriends as a youth. His mother said his violent dreams meant he needed a wife, and she had offered to arrange a marriage in accordance with their community's customs. The suggestion of marriage, even as arranged by his mother, terrorized him. He described himself as devout and had approached priests and elders for advice, but their prescription of increased prayer and meditation had little effect on this issue.

The counsellor asked the client to bring pictures, drawings, writing, or any other artifacts that would assist in understanding his self-narrative. He brought samples of his poetry. First, he would read a poem in his native language, allowing the counsellor to get a feel for the melody, and then he would provide a translation. In the poetry, women were placed on a pedestal of virtue, with men pictured as admiring, cherishing, and protecting the feminine principle. This desire to protect was long-standing. He recalled that as a child an older sister and some of her friends had begun viewing an underground copy of the movie Dracula, but he had unplugged the television when Dracula came to bite a female victim. He insisted the movie be destroyed on the threat of informing the authorities which would have led to legal consequences.

The counsellor asked the Zoroastrian client to recount his nightmares describing himself and his victims in detail including their physical characteristics. In these dreams he had no eyebrows. He was asked the significance of eyebrows in his culture. The client replied he did not know but that he would ask his mother. In the next session he informed me eyebrows are a symbol of wisdom. The counsellor blurted out, "Then it's your shadow!" and explained the figure in his dreams was not him, but a caricature of him lacking wisdom. It was explained that, according to Jung, we construct an ideal self he called our "persona"—"the good things we know we can be. The shadow consists of those parts of our selves that we have not included in our persona. I suggested that the dreams were saying that he has to come to terms with his sexual self. "But I am hurting them; I am not having sex with them," he declared. "And how would you feel if, in your dreams, you had sex with them?" he was asked. "Terrible," he replied, "it would be sinful." "Exactly," the therapist replied, "Your subconscious is protecting you by hurting that which could cause you to sin."

Human beings are meaning makers; we need to situate ourselves in a coherent worldview, and we need to feel as if our lives make sense. At this level of intervention, it is more important to provide a framework for self-understanding than to attempt to find a mechanism that is objectively true. Jung may or may not represent objective reality in this instance, but it allowed the client a new perspective for understanding his angst consistent with his prior cultural values. The new perspective allowed him to begin the task of uniting aspects of his sexuality with his already existent self. In subsequent sessions we explored aspects of his sexuality compatible with his goal of honouring women in culturally consistent ways. We began a behavioural experiment. He had been avoiding a young woman who had smiled at him in class, and indeed, he had experienced a nightmare subsequent to her smiling at him. He was encouraged to invite her to have coffee with the provision that he had to first explain to her that he just wanted friendship. To his surprise, he had a pleasant conversation with her without the usual nightmares. They went for dinner. They spent an afternoon at a zoo. He concluded he could relate to attractive women at a friendship level, and given his moral code, this was preferred prior to marriage.

---

[1] Traditionally, individuals would seek out an elder person with the knowledge they sought and offer that person tobacco and cloth as a way of commencing their special relationship. Becoming an Elder, then, was a function of the people who recognized them as such from the available pool of elders. More recently some Elders have been appointed to salaried positions by institutions such as the First Nations University of Canada.

[2] The term "Aboriginal Spirituality" is a proper noun representing a specific, defined religiously held belief system. It may be contrasted with "aboriginal spiritualities" that connote ways of understanding that are not religiously held. See: Robertson, 2014b

8

Creating Representational Visual Images

By this point the reader will know how to identify memes and support clients through the 40 persons or narrative approaches, and how to organize the memes on the map and how to make connections. We have not yet discussed how to make the visuals such as those you have seen in this manual. Both authors have experimented with different programs to make these images. Here we will discuss options and considerations in choosing a program to create your map.

While it is possible to draw the map by hand, this is not recommended due to the time and effort needed to make changes, add and remove, or relocate connections and memes. The original self-maps created to study the structure of the self used a commercial mind-mapping product by Inspiration Software Inc. This program allows the user to select a variety of shapes and move those shapes into position on a whiteboard. We chose ovals to represent memes and the program allows you to write the referent for each meme into the oval. Notes can be attached to each meme to allow easy reference to connotative, affective, and behavioural dimensions of the meme so represented. Other shapes, for example rectangles and clouds, can be used to represent thematic clusters and mini-selves. Lines of various thicknesses can be selected to represent forces of attraction or cognitive pathways. With this software program, the therapist identifies the memes, places them according to their characteristics, and shares the resultant map with the client for feedback. The therapist is then responsible for making necessary revisions.

The necessary functions for software to work for mapping include a minimum of two shapes in which text can be added, and the ability to draw lines connecting shapes. Ideally a program will be able to produce non-directional, uni-directional, and bi-directional lines. Larger curved lines that were seen in the more complex maps are useful in indicating emotional shortcuts used by the client to trigger meme clusters. Therapists can use customized symbols to represent the forces of attraction and repulsion between memes.

One of the main issues we have found is most programs, such as 'paint,' which is often included on computers, require a fair bit of time to make detailed representations two dimensions. Additionally, programs that require the clinician to complete a version of the self-map to be subsequently shared with the client can create some challenges in co-construction, especially if it is time-consuming to make changes during sessions with the client. There are, however, both free and paid web-based programs and apps that can be shared with the client and manipulated during sessions so as to allow for co-construction.

In using a web-based program, caution must be taken to protect confidentiality. This includes additional notes that might be included and how one names the map. Counsellors may use a client number and/or or initials to protect identity. Another downside to the mind-mapping applications is the need to manually rank order the memes when determining which are more central. Some online programs that are workable include Miro, Canva, and Lucidchart, all of which seem to have sufficient security by meeting the Health Insurance Portability and Accountability Act, U.S., (HIPPA) compliance but they do not advertise compliance with the Canadian Personal Information Protection and Electronic Documents Act (PIPEDA). In my (TJR) private practice, I have utilized Google Workspace and have found success using the Google Drawings feature, as of this writing, it is also compliant with PIPEDA and a good option if you already pay for the service.

We have developed the prototype of a mapping software program that will simplify the mapping process and encourage full participation on the part of the client. The program will allow clients to enter their self-descriptors and rank order them using the "Forty Persons" method. This increases the collaborative nature of the process and reduces the time therapists must spend to input the data. A benefit of the software is it automatically places the memes in their ranked order on the map, simplifying keeping those items more central to the person in the middle and the easier-to-change items can be placed around the outside. Currently the software is unable to include bi-directional arrows or thicker curved lines as we see in the more complex maps. If you are interested in keeping up to date on how this software develops, we encourage you to email us at meme@robertsonpsych.com and ask to sign up for our mailing list.

As discussed previously, the core of the client's self is comprised of those memes identified as the most important (or, alternatively, the hardest to give up). The whole structure outlines a theory that we hold to be true about ourselves, although much of it is unconscious. People do not ordinarily map themselves. What gives rise to this usually unconscious theory of self is the unspoken question after we act volitionally, "Who is doing all this stuff?" The means by which we answer this question begins with the social interactions we have experienced in childhood, supplemented by the interpretations we have placed on subsequent events. For the former, we are primarily determined beings with negative implications for individuality and will, while the latter allows for such possibilities. The mapping process described here allows us to effectively reprogram ourselves, making an encumbered free will compatible with determinism (Robertson, 2017a). The goal of increasing client participation in their own self-map construction as envisioned by this memetic software program is to increase client self-determined behaviour.

Clinicians must be aware of non-cognitive factors such as personality and heritable traits that can influence or animate the self. Sometimes psychometric assessments can be used to help inform a client of factors affecting the self; that is, making the unconscious conscious. The following seven steps are commended to clinicians using this technology to further their work:

1. Using the handout provided, participants will be asked to create four lists of who they are: ten persons that encompass roles, ten things they believe to be true, ten things they like about themselves, ten things they would change about themselves if they could;

2. The participant will be asked to rank order each item on each list from the most important to least important. The clinician and participant co-construct code-names or labels representing each item;
3. The clinician explores connotative, affective and behavioural characteristics associated with each named item with the client. Those items that have all three characteristics are declared to be memes;
4. The clinician and participant then co-construct the memetic map by sharing visuals between sessions and adding to the maps in sessions (it may be helpful to print what you have so connections can be drawn and new memes added during sessions). Memes that have been prioritized as more important by the participant are placed more centrally on their self-map. Memes that share characteristics (connotative, affective or behavioural) are considered linked. Those that lead behaviourally to other memes are also considered linked and this connection is represented by edges connecting memes;
5. Groups of memes that may act in concert when triggered (as in a script), or may present as a "mini-self" in particular contexts or otherwise present as a group are identified and given a thematic label;
6. The clinicians and participants explore personality characteristics, traumas, illnesses and other predispositions that may trigger meme clusters but are not part of the conscious self represented by memes. These are summarized and placed at the bottom of the self-map with directional edges connecting the base characteristics with associated meme clusters;
7. The self-map is reviewed for participant resonance, that is, the participant subjectively feels the map represents who they are. Each participant is asked to review the map for changes that might increase this feeling of resonance.

9

Limitations and Concluding Thoughts

Clinicians may generate new techniques during the course of psychotherapy when established treatments fail. The method developed here was first used to treat a youth who was experiencing suicidal ideation that was resistant to antidepressant medication, cognitive behavioural therapy, Adlerian psychotherapy, and eye movement reprocessing and desensitization (Robertson, 2011). Using the narrative method of generating memes, the practice of memetic self-mapping was tested on a qualitative cross-cultural sample of people who were not in psychotherapy (Robertson, 2009). Subsequent research has consisted of published case studies and the reports of the authors in their practices. We need to confirm our anecdotal findings in larger studies using mixed methods. While we believe the methods of generating self-maps described here are compatible with various schools of psychotherapy, research demonstrating efficacy across this range of schools has not been done. In addition, research using the self-mapping technique on targeted populations whose selves have been damaged by trauma, psychiatric illness, or other life experiences is indicated.

Two methods of identifying memes for self-mapping were described here. The "forty persons" method used to create figure 4 appears to be more directive than the narrative method used to create figure 8. Research is indicated to demonstrate the equivalency of these two methods. Research may assess the efficacy of methods as applied to research and use in therapy sessions. It is possible, using the "Forty Persons" method, that the failure to identify such an emotional base is a methodological oversight.

While there may be a basic structure to the self, the importance placed on certain aspects of that structure and their relationship to other aspects of the self would be expected to vary between cultures. Memetic mapping may be used to further study how the selves in various cultures are constituted. As we have seen, the dichotomy between collectivist and individualist is simplistic, as the self is constituted and maintained by social forces in all cultures. The study of cultural differences will include consideration of how such forces are accommodated, balanced, and interpreted.

Memetic mapping is a technique and, as such, is subject to influence by each practitioner's style and preferred therapeutic approaches. While we support the view that the process aligns with a number of common approaches, we are limited in that practitioners currently using it share commonality in approaches and client demographics. Data gathered by therapists with a broad range of focuses and approaches would demonstrate how transferable the mapping methods are. Given that memetic mapping uses supported psychotherapy skills incorporated into existing therapeutic frameworks, the risks in applying the technique in therapy are low.

In applying memetic mapping, the only research conducted to date is by the lead author (LHR) who developed the process. Study replication and greater sample sizes would show the efficacy of memetic mapping as a technique and encourage further research and refinement of the methods. It is our hope that memetic mapping has enough perceived utility for therapy that psychotherapists will want to learn the technique and further the research.

Conclusions

To review, we are utilizing the meme as the smallest replicating unit of culture within an individual, and we illustrate the relationship between memes in map form. We identify memes by using either the 40 persons or the narrative approach and place them in relation to each other using shared qualities between them. Once the individual client resonates with the mapped representation of themselves, we collaboratively explore patterns that lead to maladaptive recurrent behaviours. We consider additional factors such as hereditable traits, psychological characteristics, personality, and environmental variables and how they affect the individual. The therapist looks for the seven core elements, rumination cycles, themes, and adaptive parts that need to be strengthened, all while taking into consideration the client's readiness to change. Often the client will spontaneously suggest self changes upon review of his or her map. It is often best to focus first on strengthening adaptive parts that are already present to minimize risks of destabilizing the client's sense of self. Changes that are made can then be reflected in the map, as it evolves with the client.

As we have hopefully demonstrated, memetic self-mapping is not a hard and fast rigid technique. The process is adaptable to the therapist and client's style and needs. Sometimes mapping is the only thing focused on in therapy; other times it is completed alongside specific goals and tools being worked on in sessions where the memes and map help the client and therapist notice the patterns that keep them stuck in problematic patterns of thinking and behaviour. It might take 3 sessions to have a first draft, and it might take 8, all depending on how it is used and how complex one wants to make it. While the overarching way the map is created is structured, how it is used therapeutically or what it looks like to co-construct the map is not.

The authors are interested in further refining the approach and collaborating with other therapists utilizing this tool. Whether you have questions, ideas, comments, or concerns or are engaging in research using the technique, we want to hear about your experiences. Handouts and updates can be found at: www.robertsonpsych.com/memetic-mapping in the drop-down. Questions should be addressed through email to: meme@robertsonpsych.com. You may also opt in to a mailing list for updates, training offers, and discussion groups. We are also open to paid consultation to help teach and work with you on implementing this technique.

Appendix A

Appendix A: A Sample of How Text was Segmented and Coded for the Meme "Mother" in Building Tina's Self-Map

A transcript of Tina's initial interview was divided into 52 segments and each segment was given at least one code word identifying a key aspect of the segment. The segments coded with the same words were then grouped together in the same "bin," and emergent characteristics were examined in comparison with the structure used in defining meme, and words satisfying that definition were retained as memes. Eleven of the segments from Tina's initial transcript were coded for the meme "mother." Those eleven segments are reproduced here along with the rationale for defining "mother" in the way it was presented and for the connections between "mother" and other memes.

Segment #5 coded for "mother" and "self-changer"

In answer to the question, "What made you change (to stop partying)?" Tina answered, *"Having kids, you have no choice but to grow up.... The first one fell in my lap, so I didn't plan the first one; he just kind of dropped in my lap, I guess you could say."*

Notes: A meme for "self-changer" was not added until after Tina's second interview, when she developed the idea of changing herself into a self-defining meme. As an example, after she discovered she was pregnant with her first child, she decided to become more responsible and not "party." She explained that any "decent" expectant mother would have done the same.

Segment #14 coded for "animator" and "mother"

"I get compliments, people telling me, "Oh, you've got such really good kids, well mannered," and they never say, "What?" they always say, "Pardon me, please and thank you," we're really hard on them, really strict. We don't let them do much, not as much as, like they wanna go play in the bush. They can't do that. I used to be able to when I was a kid, but I won't let my kids go in there. I just.. they always have to be around me to make sure I know they're safe, and, yeah, I'm very proud of the way they turned out."

Notes: This segment is about Tina's role as a mother, but it also places her in control over her children. This suggested a link between "mother" and "animator." This segment connotes motherhood with responsibility, and behaviourally she is responsible for their safety. The phrase "they always have to be around me" may imply anxiety, although the segment itself is not about anxiety.

Segment #33 coded for "independent belief," "mother" and "sister"

"I have pictures of (a son that died of crib death) and I have pictures of (a sister who died two years after she met her) all over the house, and I don't think he (her father) likes that, but I don't care I don't take them down."

Notes: This segment suggests a link between Tina's role as a mother and her assertion of independent belief to her father. "Mother" and "Sister" were linked thematically through "Love" and "Family Person."

Segment #34 coded for "paranoid" and "mother"

"I only got to know my son for 6 months and 25 days and I only knew my sister for 2 years, so yeah, you take every moment in. I think that's why I'm so paranoid with him (her newest baby) as well, he won't sleep by himself, I have a baby heart monitor and a breath monitor. I just won't leave him alone."

Notes: This segment suggested a link between "paranoid" and "mother." The suggestion of parental responsibility and the need to ensure her child's safety is made.

Segment #35 coded for "paranoid" and "mother"

"There's nothing gonna happen to him, nothing at all. The only thing I don't have is a video camera monitor, and actually that's something I'm thinking about getting too, so he can sleep in the room by himself without me freaking out going in there every 5 minutes so.

Notes: The link between "paranoid" and "mother" was reinforced along with a responsibility to ensure that "nothing is gonna happen...."

Segment #38 coded for "daughter," "mother," "sister," and "wife."

"Love for my kids, the way I feel about my mom and dad, sister, brother, husband my kids, and uh, the way I love them and take care of them, pamper them, make sure they're ok, I don't think that will ever change about myself, I'll always have that, that bond with them, and I don't think that will ever change."

Notes: This segment tied Tina's roles as daughter, mother, sister, and wife together with the themes of love and family.

Segment #42 coded for "mother"

"I take the kids out, if they're nice. I don't spoil them to the fact that I give them whatever they want, but they do have a lot of stuff that a lot of kids don't have, like games and systems like they probably have every game system available, except for PlayStation. They got 2 Xboxes, 1 Xbox 360, a computer in their room - they just have lots of stuff lots and lots of stuff"

Notes: This segment speaks to her role as a mother. She wants to shape their behaviour, not spoil them, but ensure that they have toys, games and computers

Segment #43 coded for "mother" and "reader"

"I read to them all the time, and if they don't have a new book to read they get bored easy and they have shelves, shelves and shelves of book's from when I was little, that I read to them all the time, and I continually have to buy books, cause they need to read different stories and stuff like that. They are, I guess I'm being a lot like my dad spoiling my kids that way too."

Notes: This segment suggests that it is a parental responsibility to read to children. The link between "mother" and "reader" was missed during the construction of Tina's map.

Segment #44 coded for "education" and "mother"

"I'm very, very hard on my kids. Most kids come home, and a lot of parents don't care. They let them do whatever, go play games. My kids aren't allowed to have friends during the weekday. They have to come home do their chores, do their homework, have a bath, get ready for bed, go to bed."

Notes: This segment refers to parental responsibilities to ensure that children are provided with a lifestyle conducive to their success in school and in learning to be responsible. The parental role includes caring for their children and ensuring that their lifestyle needs are met.

Segment #45 coded for "mother"

"They're just constantly "Mom, mom, mom, let's do this, can I go to the grocery store with you? Can I do this with you?" and like my 6 year old likes to make a groceries list. We always did that. I made half the list, and he makes half the list and I send him off to the grocery store. He'll go and get whatever is on the list, and stuff like that. He's pretty good at that, but we haven't been doing much of that lately 'cause I have to make sure he's fed, and then I have to go rush to the grocery store, and when I'm in the grocery store, that's when I usually have a panic attack, 'cause then I'm usually thinking, "Oh, I gotta go home, what If he's crying? what if he's freaking out? He can't cry for so long." and then, so a lot of time, he doesn't get to go with me 'cause I'm in a rush, rush mode, and I have to try and rush to get home.

Notes: This segment speaks to parental responsibilities for teaching children to be responsible and to ensure they are fed. Reference to a "panic attack" coupled with questions about whether or not he may be crying was interpreted as providing evidence of a link to anxiety.

Segment #47 coded for "education" and "mother"

"Like he always does his homework he's sits there and do his homework for 2 hours after school, and most kids won't even do that, and he will and… 'cause you have to be on a schedule and stuff like that. My 6 year old he's not into homework yet, but next year it will be starting.

Notes: This segment links education with the role as mother to support that education. A link between "education" and "mother" is suggested along with a maternal responsibility coupled with behaviours to support their education.

Appendix B

Appendix B: The Memes Used in Building Tina's Self-Showing Referent, Connotative, Emotive and Behavioural Components:

The terms that are flush left in bold refer to interpretive themes and they are followed by the memes that led to those interpretive codes. The terms that are flush left without being highlighted in bold were identified as memes. Terms may be memes and themes simultaneously, in which case they are in bold but followed with referent, connotative, affective and behavioural descriptions. The numbers beside the memes record the number of segments coded for a particular meme that appeared in the transcript of the first interview.

Family Person (interpretive theme)
Love
Mediator (1)
REFERENT: Mediates between family members to resolve conflict
CONNOTATION: Role as peacemaker, associated with being open-minded
AFFECT: Caring for others
BEHAVIOUR: Listens to others, talks to them about feelings, helps them to see other points of view

Sister (5)
REFERENT: Having brothers and sisters
CONNOTATION: Siblings are very important
AFFECT: Caring, love
BEHAVIOUR: Embraces siblings, including a sister she had not known

Daughter (3)
REFERENT: Has biological parents
CONNOTATION: Implies duty such as caring for, cleaning
AFFECT: Love
BEHAVIOUR: Cleans house for parents, ensures they have food

Mother (11)
REFERENT: A biological fact associated with bearing children
CONNOTATION: Maternal responsibility to those children to shape their behaviour and ensure their future success
AFFECT: Love, caring, valuing of children
BEHAVIOUR: Ensures that her children are safe, cared for, read to, go to school, are given toys

Anxious (2)
REFERENT: Suffers from anxiety/panic attacks (1-2 times per month)
CONNOTATION: There is something wrong with her
AFFECT: Distress
BEHAVIOUR: Goes by herself and talks herself out of bouts of panic/anxiety

Blamer (1)
REFERENT: To identify and hold responsible those responsible for wrong-doing
CONNOTATION: Tina has the right to hold others, even her parents, responsible for their actions
AFFECT: Anger
BEHAVIOUR: Blames parents for not accepting her half-sister, blames self for the crib-death of one son

Paranoid (4)
REFERENT: Excessive concern over the safety of her children
CONNOTATION: Mothers are responsible when bad things happen to their children
AFFECT: Worry
BEHAVIOUR: Monitors children continually, won't allow them to play in the bush behind their house

Not in Shape (2)
REFERENT: Overweight
CONNOTATION: Not attractive
AFFECT: Disappointment, mild disgust directed toward her body
BEHAVIOUR: Wishful, plans future activities to get in shape

Wife (9)
REFERENT: The spouse of a husband
CONNOTATION: Must cater to her husband
AFFECT: Love, purpose, pride (in relationship)
BEHAVIOUR: Cooks, cleans, manicures her husband

Cleaner (5)
REFERENT: Cleans, straightens
CONNOTATION: By cleaning, she is a good person
AFFECT: Feeling of pride, accomplishment
BEHAVIOUR: Compulsively cleans homes—her own, her parents, friends

Budgeter (2)

REFERENT: To plan for the use of limited resources
CONNOTATION: Is responsible, can make adequate determinations
AFFECT: Purpose and pride
BEHAVIOUR: Pays bills, budgets for family, organizes resources for extra-curricular activities for children, organizes resources to provide for her children

Decent Person
Caring (3)
REFERENT: A feeling that suggests the well-being of others is important to oneself
CONNOTATION: Decent people care about others
AFFECT: A feeling of closeness and responsibility for others
BEHAVIOUR: Cares for parents by taking care of their needs, doesn't like mean people who stereotype, describes self as decent and caring

Open Minded (5)
REFERENT: Accepts people of different cultural and religious beliefs, orientations and practices
CONNOTATION: All people are good; open-minded with a willingness to talk about feelings; decent people are open-minded
AFFECT: Easy-going acceptance
BEHAVIOUR: Welcomes people of different religious perspectives, sexual orientations, cultures into her home; accepts that her husband may have additional (but approved) sexual liaisons

Kids (1)
REFERENT: Young humans who are not yet adults
CONNOTATION: Children have primary importance
AFFECT: Loves all children
BEHAVIOUR: Welcomes all children into her home, takes children in who have no place to live

Outgoing (2)
REFERENT: Willing to interact with others in an open way
CONNOTATION: People may be trusted to the degree necessary for honest interaction
AFFECT: Liking others
BEHAVIOUR: Welcomes others into her home, will talk to and show friendliness to others

Guy Friends (1)
REFERENT: Has more male friends than female
CONNOTATION: Men are easier to get along with
AFFECT: Feels comfortable around men
BEHAVIOUR: Relates more readily to men (except for lesbian and bisexual women)

Anti-stereotyping (1)
REFERENT: Judging others based on some external criteria
CONNOTATION: Decent people do not stereotype others
AFFECT: Doesn't like people who stereotype, feelings are deepened by the experience of having been stereotyped by teachers, strait women
BEHAVIOUR: Engages verbally with those who stereotype including teachers who have preconceived notions about how a particular student should perform

Gay Friends (1)
REFERENT: Having homosexual/bisexual friends
CONNOTATION: Being open-minded she values others for who they are
AFFECT: Pride in being more open-minded than others in the community
BEHAVIOUR: Cultivates gay friends, defends their right to be who they are

Empowered
Animator (2)
REFERENT: Believes that she can carry out plans to achieve goals
CONNOTATION: Doing and being responsible shows importance, implies security
AFFECT: Feeling of place, responsibility for people for whom she cares
BEHAVIOUR: Takes responsibility for certain tasks, controls the conduct of her children, cleans, budgets, shops

Learner
Education (4)
REFERENT: Formal learning as defined by the education system
CONNOTATION: A good mother pursues what is important for her children
AFFECT: Pride, responsibility
BEHAVIOUR: Insists her children have good study and homework habits

Reader (2)
REFERENT: Someone who reads
CONNOTATION: Reading is a valuable activity
AFFECT: Desire to read, and to ensure her children read
BEHAVIOUR: Reads to her children, ensures that they read at home as well as at school

Independent Belief (1)
REFERENT: To have believes different from others, particularly family of origin
CONNOTATION: Makes getting along with others easier, means talking about one's feelings
AFFECT: Positive feeling about self

BEHAVIOUR: Welcomes others of differing views, cultures, orientations

Stubborn (1)
REFERENT: Obstinate and unmoving in certain opinions
CONNOTATION: Likes own way, implied self-centeredness
AFFECT: Unease with connotative meanings of "stubborn"
BEHAVIOUR: Insists on getting her way about things that matter to her, particularly with respect to her children, holds on to cherished belief

Memes Added After the Second Interview

Yeller
REFERENT: One who yells to enforce compliance
CONNOTATION: She will not be listened to by her children if she talks to them in her normal voice and has less authority, therefore, than her husband
AFFECT: Frustration
BEHAVIOUR: Continues to admonish her children in a loud voice when she wants to be taken seriously

Self-Changer
REFERENT: One who consciously and deliberately makes changes to the self
CONNOTATION: She is in control of who she becomes
AFFECT: Empowerment
BEHAVIOUR: Is making changes with respect to her roles as wife, mother, smoker, and paranoid

Assertive
REFERENT: One who expresses thoughts and feelings appropriately in a way that they are heard.
CONNOTATION: Those thoughts and feelings are worthy of expression
AFFECT: Satisfaction
BEHAVIOUR: Is asserting needs to family

Pleaser
REFERENT: Looks after others' needs to the exclusion of her own
CONNOTATION: She is a good or decent person when she puts others' needs ahead of her own
AFFECT: Anger and frustration when her own needs are neglected
BEHAVIOUR: Cries, usually in private, when her own needs are not met

Hider of Negative Feelings

REFERENT: Hides negative emotions from others
CONNOTATION: Negative feelings are bad, and it is her duty to prevent others from seeing such unpleasantness.
AFFECT: Aloneness
BEHAVIOUR: Will hide in her room when feeling down.

Bisexual
REFERENT: A person who is sexually attracted to both sexes
CONNOTATION: Thinks "like a guy," finds that women "play head games."
AFFECT: Feeling of separateness from most women
BEHAVIOUR: Role plays expected behaviours for "straight" women, but defends sexual minorities (gays, bisexuals)

Role-player
REFERENT: To play a role appropriate to a given context
CONNOTATION: She would not be accepted if some women knew her "true" self; there is a true or essential self
AFFECT: Feels uncomfortable while playing a role, feels more comfortable with men generally
BEHAVIOUR: Plays the role of "straight" with straight women

Handouts

Appendix C: Handouts

The following handouts support the mapping process.

1. **40 persons**: This handout is intended for the client to complete either in session or on their own between sessions, to then review with the therapist and be given a name/descriptor. At this stage you may use the "Is it a meme?" handout to check that each contains the 4 components of a meme.

2. **Is it a meme?** The purpose of this is to support analysis of each meme name and check that it includes the 4 components. If it does not it is not a meme. This tool may help in identifying repetitive memes that may be combined into one. The client may start it on their own or work on it with the clinician.

3. **7 core memes:** prompts to check if these memes are present or missing.

40 Persons

For each section, come up with at least 10 answers (there are extra spaces as needed). Once you have completed a section, please rank them from 1 (easiest to change or give up) to 10+ (hardest to change or give up).

Name at least 10 persons you are:

-
-
-
-
-
-

-
-
-
-
-
-

Name at least 10 things you believe to be true:

-
-
-
-
-

-
-
-
-
-

Name at least 10 things you would change about yourself if you could:

-
-
-
-
-
-

-
-
-
-
-
-

Name at least 10 things you like about yourself:

-
-
-
-
-

-
-
-
-
-

Is it a meme?

For each potential meme, explore if it involves the 4 components. Referent: what is it; Connotation: meaning to the individual; Affect: emotions attached; Behaviour: actions or things one does because of the meme.

Ex) MEME: Anxious
REFERENT: Suffers from anxiety/panic attacks (1-2 times per month)
CONNOTATION: There is something wrong with her
AFFECT: Distress
BEHAVIOUR: Goes by herself and talks herself out of bouts of panic/anxiety

Meme:
Referent:
Connotation:
Affect:
Behaviour:

Meme:
Referent:
Connotation:
Affect:
Behaviour:

Meme:
Referent:
Connotation:
Affect:
Behaviour:

Meme:
Referent:
Connotation:
Affect:
Behaviour:

Meme:

Referent:
Connotation:
Affect:
Behaviour:

Meme:
Referent:
Connotation:
Affect:
Behaviour:

Meme:
Referent:
Connotation:
Affect:
Behaviour:

Meme:
Referent:
Connotation:
Affect:
Behaviour:

Meme:
Referent:
Connotation:
Affect:
Behaviour:

Constancy: What exists in the self regardless of space and time. What is always a part of them? If we cannot see it, are there values that have always been important to them, do they persist even if actions don't always align?

Individual volition: Does the person see themselves as someone who can affect change in their life? Using simple behavioural experiments to see the effects of choices can be powerful in increasing volition. For instance, if they do self-care, something enjoyable, or connect with a friend, how does it impact their mood?

Uniqueness: What indication or feeling is there that they are different than others? If this is lacking, how can we help them to connect with the feeling of uniqueness, e.g., love? They are the only ones feeling that exact feeling about that person in that moment.

Productivity: Are they achieving or contributing to something? Do they view this as meaningful or productive in their life? What do they do in a day? Who does it affect and what does that affect mean to them?

Intimacy: Are there indications of meaningful relationships and connections to others? Who do they feel close to? Or who could they make efforts to build more closeness to? Are they a part of a group that makes them feel connected?

Remembering/reflecting: Is there indication that they remember stories, transitions, different parts of their lives, and that they can reflect on themselves?

Social interest: In what ways do they view themselves as contributing to something greater than themselves? This is often a missing piece- can have them engage in a social way to contribute to an area that matters to them (volunteering, board member, public works, advocacy, etc.).

References

Adler, A. (1927/1957). *Understanding human nature* (B. Wolfe, Trans.). Fawcett. (1927)

Adler, A. (1929). *The science of living*. Greenberg, Publisher.

Atran, S. (2002). *In gods we trust: The evolutionary landscape of religion*. Oxford University Press.

Bassett, D. S., & Bullmore, E. (2006). Small-world brain networks. *Neuroscience, 12*(6), 512-523. https://doi.org/10.1177/1073858406293182

Battaglia, D. (1995). Problematizing the self: A thematic introduction. In D. Battaglia (Ed.), *Rhetorics of self-making* (pp. 1-15). University of California Press.

Baumeister, R. F., Campbell, J. D., Krueger, J. I., & Vohs, K. D. (2004). *Exploding the self-esteem myth*. Retrieved February 24 from http://www.sciam.com/article.cfm?articleID=000CB565-F330-11BE-AD0683414B7F0000&sc=I100322

Bhogal, G. S. (2023). Why Smart People Believe Stupid Things; Intelligence Is Not Rationality. *The Prism*. Retrieved February 15, 2023, from https://gurwinder.substack.com/p/why-smart-people-hold-stupid-beliefs?utm_source=ActiveCampaign&utm_medium=email&utm_content=A+Chemical+Train+Derailment+in+Ohio&utm_campaign=A+Chemical+Train+Derailment+in+Ohio

Blackmore, S. (1999). *The meme machine*. Oxford University Press.

Blustein, D. L., & Noumair, A. (1996). Self and identity in career development: Implications for theory and practice. *Journal of Counseling & Development, 74*(5), 433-452. <http://80-web25.epnet.com.ezproxy.lib.ucalgary.ca:2048/citation.asp>

Brasfield, C. R. (2001). Residential School Syndrome. *B.C. Medical Journal, 43*(2), 78-81.

Burman, J. T. (2012). The misunderstanding of memes: Biography of an unscientific object, 1976 - 1999. *Perspectives on Science, 20*(1), 75-104.

Coyne, J. A. (2012). You don't have free will. *The Chronicle of Higher Education, 18*, 21.

Csikszentmihalyi, M. (1993). *The evolving self: A psychology for the third millennium*. Harper Collins.

Cull, J. G., & Gill, W. S. (1988). *Suicide Probability Scale (SPS) manual*. Western Psychological Services.

Damasio, A. (1999). *The feeling of what happens: Body and emotion in the making of consciousness*. Harcourt.

Damon, W., & Hart, D. (1988). *Self-understanding in childhood and adolescence*. Cambridge University Press.

Dawkins, R. (1976). *The selfish gene*. Oxford University Press.

Dawkins, R. (1986). *The blind watchmaker*. Penguin Books.

De Man, A. F., & Gutierrez, B. I. (2002). The relationship between level of self-esteem and suicidal ideation with stability of self-esteem as moderator. *Canadian Journal of Behavioural Science, 34*(4), 235-238. https://doi.org/10.1037/h0087176

Dennett, D. C. (1995). *Darwin's dangerous idea: Evolution and the meanings of life*. Simon and Schuster.

Dennett, D. C. (1996). *Kinds of minds: Toward an understanding of consciousness*. Harper Collins.

Dinkmeyer, D. C., Pew, W. L., & Dinkmeyer, D. C. J. (1979). *Adlerian counselling and psychotherapy*. Brooks / Cole.

Donald, M. (2001). *A mind so rare: The evolution of human consciousness*. Norton.

Dozois, D. (2002, October 5, 6). *Cognitive therapy in clinical depression: Structure, specificity and stability* First Annual Meeting of the Institute of Neurosciences, Mental Health and Addictions, Montreal.

Dozois, D., & Dobson, K. S. (2001). Information processing and cognitive organization in unipolar depression: Specificity and comorbidity issues. *Journal of Abnormal Psychology, 110*(2), 236-246. https://doi.org/10.1037/0021-843X.110.2.236

Dryden, W., Neenan, M., & Yankura, J. (2001). *Counselling individuals: A rational emotive behavioural handbook* (3 ed.). Whurr Publishers.

Freidman, D., & Sing, N. (2004). Negative reciprocity: The co-evolution of memes and genes. *Evolution and Human Behavior, 25*(3), 155-173.

Fritz, G. K. (2007). Looking for evidence in evidenced-based medicine: Antidepressants and the risk of suicide. *Brown University Child & Adolescent Behavior Letter*, 8. http://search.ebscohost.com/login.aspx?direct=true&db=a2h&AN=25060198&site=ehost-live

Gazzaniga, M. S. (2000). Cerebral specialization and interhemispheric communication: Does the corpus callosum enable the human condition? . *Brain, 137*(7), 1293-1326. https://doi.org/10.1093/brain/123.7.1293

Glaser, B. G. (1992). *Basics of grounded theory analysis: Emergence vs forcing*. Sociology Press.

Heath, C., Bell, C., & Sternberg, E. (2001). Emotional selection in memes: The case of urban legends. *Journal of Personality & Social Psychology, 81*(6), 1028-1041.

Hinton, D. E., & Kirmayer, L. J. (2016). The Flexibility Hypothesis of Healing. *Culture, Medicine, and Psychiatry*, 1-32. https://doi.org/10.1007/s11013-016-9493-8

Hvid, M., & Wang, A. G. (2009). Preventing repetition of attempted suicide: Feasibility (acceptability, adherence, and effectiveness) of a Baerum-model like aftercare. *Nordic Journal of Psychiatry, 63*(2), 148-153. 10.1080/08039480802423022
http://search.ebscohost.com/login.aspx?direct=true&db=a2h&AN=37185785&site=ehost-live

Hyer, L., Kramer, D., & Sohnle, S. (2004). CBT with Older People: Alterations and the Value of the Therapeutic Alliance. *Psychotherapy: Theory, Research, Practice, Training, 41*(3), 276-291.

Kanis, H. (2004). The quantitative-qualitative research dichotomy revisited. *Theoretical Issues in Ergonomics Science, 5*(6), 507-516.

James, W. (1890). *The principles of psychology* (Vol. 1). Macmillan.

Jaspers, K. (1951). *Way to Wisdom: An Introduction to Philosophy*. Yale University Press.

Jaynes, J. (1976). *The origins of consciousness in the breakdown of the bicameral mind*. Houghton Mifflin.

Johnson, D. M. (2003). *How history made mind: The cultural origins of objective thinking*. Open Court Books.

Karver, M., Shirk, S., Handelsman, J. B., Fields, S., Crisp, H., Gudmundsen, G., & McMakin, D. (2008). Relationship Processes in Youth Psychotherapy: Measuring Alliance, Alliance-Building Behaviors, and Client Involvement. *Journal of Emotional & Behavioral Disorders, 16*(1), 15-28. https://doi.org/10.1177/1063426607312536

Korhonen, M.-L. (2002). *Inuit clients and the effective helper: An investigation of culturally sensitive counselling* University of Durham]. Durham, UK.

Leary, M., & Tangney, J. P. (2003). The self as an organizing construct in the behavioral and social sciences. In M. Leary & J. P. Tangney (Eds.), *Handbook of self and identity* (pp. 3-14). Gilford Press.

Lightsey, O. R., Boyraz, G., Ervin, A., Rarey, E. B., Gharghani, G. G., & Maxwell, D. (2014). Generalized self-efficacy, positive cognitions, and negative cognitions as mediators of the relationship between conscientiousness and meaning in life. *Canadian Journal of Behavioural Science, 46*(3), 436-445. https://doi.org/10.1037/a0034022

Louisy, H. J. (1996). *Core beliefs assessment procedure: The development of a cognitive-behavioural case formulation method* University of Saskatchewan]. Saskatoon, SK.

Mahoney, M. J. (1991). *Human change processes: The scientific foundations of psychotherapy*. Basic Books.

Maniacci, M. P., Sackett-Maniacci, L., & Mosak, H. H. (2014). Adlerian Psychotherapy. In D. Wedding & R. J. Corsini (Eds.), *Current Psychotherapies* (10 ed.). Brooks / Cole.

McAdams, D. P. (2012). Meaning and personality. In P. T. P. Wong (Ed.), *The human quest for meaning: Theories, research, and applications* (2 ed., pp. 107-123). Routledge.

Mead, G. H. (1912/1990). The mechanisms of social consciousness. In J. Pickering & M. Skinner (Eds.), *From sentience to symbols: Readings on consciousness* (pp. 192-197). University of Toronto Press.

Miles, M. B., & Huberman, A. M. (1994). *Qualitative data analysis: An expanded sourcebook* (2 ed.). Sage.

Neimeyer, R. A. (2002). The relational co-construction of selves: A postmodern perspective. *Journal of Contemporary Psychotherapy, 32*(1), 51-59.

Pinker, S. (1997). *How the mind works*. Norton.

Pinker, S. (2021). *Rationality: What is is, why it seems scarce, why it matters*. Penguin.

Quinn, N. (2011). Models school reconsidered: A paradigm shift in cognitive anthropology. In D. B. Kronenfeld, G. Bennardo, V. C. d. Munc, & M. D. Fische (Eds.), *A companion to cognitive anthropology* (Vol. 1, pp. 30-47). Blackwell.

Robertson, L. H. (2006). The residential school experience: Syndrome or historic trauma. *Pimatisiwin: A Journal of Aboriginal and Indigenous Community Health, 4*(1), 1-28.

Robertson, L. H. (2009). *The memetic self: Understanding the self using a visual mapping technique* University of Calgary]. Calgary, AB.

Robertson, L. H. (2010). Mapping the self with units of culture. *Psychology, 1*(3), 185-193. https://doi.org/10.4236/psych.2010.13025

Robertson, L. H. (2011). Self-mapping in treating suicide ideation: A case study. *Death Studies, 35*(3), 267-280. https://doi.org/10.1080/07481187.2010.496687

Robertson, L. H. (2014a). In search of the aboriginal self: Four individual perspectives. *SAGE Open, 4*(2), 1-13. https://doi.org/10.1177/2158244014534246

Robertson, L. H. (2014b). Native Spirituality: The making of a new religion. *Humanist Perspectives, 47(1)*(1), 30-37.

Robertson, L. H. (2015). The trauma of colonization: A psycho-historical analysis of one aboriginal community in the North American "North-West" *Interamerican Journal of Psychology, 49*(3), 317-332.

Robertson, L. H. (2016). Self-mapping in counselling: Using memetic maps to enhance client reflectivity and therapeutic efficacy. *Canadian Journal of Counselling and Psychotherapy, 50*(3), 332-347.

Robertson, L. H. (2017a). Implications of a culturally evolved self for notions of free will [Hypothesis and Theory]. *Frontiers in Psychology, 8*(1889), 1-8. https://doi.org/10.3389/fpsyg.2017.01889

Robertson, L. H. (2017b). The infected self: Revisiting the metaphor of the mind virus. *Theory & Psychology, 27*(3), 354-368. https://doi.org/10.1177/0959354317696601

Robertson, L. H. (2018). Male Stigma: Emotional and behavioral effects of a negative social identity on a group of Canadian men. *American Journal of Men's Health, 12*(4), 1118-1130. https://doi.org/10.1177/1557988318763661

Robertson, L. H. (2020). *The Evolved Self: Mapping an understanding of who we are*. University of Ottawa Press.

Robertson, L. H. (2021). The Medicine Wheel Revisited: Reflections on Indigenization in Counseling and Education. *SAGE Open, 11*(2), 1-11. https://doi.org/10.1177/21582440211015202

Robertson, L. H., Holleran, K., & Samuels, M. (2015). Tailoring university counselling services to aboriginal and international students: Lessons from native and international student centres at a Canadian university. *Canadian Journal of Higher Education, 45*(1), 122-135.

Robertson, L. H., & McFadden, R. C. (2018). Graphing the Self: An application of graph theory to memetic self-mapping in psychotherapy. *International and Multidisciplinary Journal of Social Sciences, 7*(1), 34-58. https://doi.org/10.17583/rimcis.2018.3078

Robertson, L. H., Robertson, T. J., & Robertson, D. T. (2020). The opened mind: An application of the historical concept of openness to education. In D. Conrad & P. Prinsloo (Eds.), *Opening education: Theory and practice* (pp. 26-46). Brill. https://doi.org/org/10.1163/9789004422988

Robertson, L. H., & Robertson, T. (2024). The Evolved Self: Mapping an Understanding of the Self in Psychotherapy. *Athens Journal of Psychology, 1*, 1-17. https://www.athensjournals.gr/psychology/2023-5337-AJPSY-PSY-Robertson-02.pdf

Robles-Diaz-de-Leon, L. F. (2003). *A memetic / participatory approach for changing social behavior and promoting environmental stewardship in Jalisco, Mexico* University of Maryland]. College Park, MD, US.

Rodebaugh, T. L., & Chambless, D. L. (2004). Cognitive therapy for performance anxiety. *Journal of Clinical Psychology, 60*(8), 809-821.

Ryum, T., & Stiles, T. C. (2005). The predictive validity of therapeutic alliance for outcome in psychotherapy: A pilot study. *Tidsskrift for Norsk Psykologforening, 42*(11), 998-1003.

Seth, A. (2021). *Being you: A new science of consciousness*. Penguin.

Shotter, J. (1997). The social construction of our inner selves. *Journal of Constructivist Psychology, 10*(1), 7-24.

Strauss, A. L. (1987). *Qualitative analysis for social scientists*. Cambridge University Press.

Tippett, L. J., Prebble, S. C., & Addis, D. R. (2018). The Persistence of the Self over Time in Mild Cognitive Impairment and Early Alzheimer's Disease. *Frontiers in Psychology, 9*, 94. https://doi.org/10.3389/fpsyg.2018.00094/full

Tsang, W. H. W., Mau, T., Chan, S., Shen, A. C.-T., & Chen, J.-S. (2023). Chinese male survivors of intimate partner violence: living in and transforming stigma. *Social Work Practice*. https://doi.org/https://doi.org/10.1080/02650533.2023.2234630

Waldram, J. B. (2004). *Revenge of the Windigo: The construction of the mind and mental health of North American aboriginal peoples*. University of Toronto Press.

Waldram, J. B. (2014). Healing history? Aboriginal healing, historical trauma, and personal responsibility. *Transcultural psychiatry, 51*(3), 370-386. https://doi.org/10.1177/1363461513487671

Wampold, B. E. (2000). Outcomes of individual counselling and psychotherapy: Empirical evidence addressing two fundamental questions. In S. D. Brown & R. W. Lent (Eds.), *Handbook of current psychotherapies* (pp. 711-739).

Wang, J., & Lin, E. (2008). An alternative interpretation of the relationship between self-concept and mathematics achievement: Comparison of Chinese and US students as a context. *Evaluation & Research in Education, 21*(3), 154-174. https://doi.org/10.1080/09500790802485203

Warwar, S., & Greenberg, L. S. (2000). Advances in theories of change and counselling. In S. D. Brown & R. W. Lent (Eds.), *Handbook of counselling psychology* (3rd ed., pp. 571-600). Wiley and Sons.

Watts, D. J., & Strogatz, S. H. (1998). Collective dynamics of 'small-world' networks. *Nature, 393*(6684), 440-442.

Wesley-Esquimaux, C. C., & Smolewski, M. (2004). *Historic trauma and aboriginal healing*. Aboriginal Healing Foundation.

About the Authors

Dr. Lloyd Hawkeye Robertson is a psychologist in private practice and an Adjunct Professor of Psychology at the University of Regina. His main professional interest has been on the evolution and structure of the self.

He has also published on the psychological impacts of Indian residential schools, the use of a community development process to combat youth suicide, the construction of the (North American) aboriginal self, the concept of free will in psychotherapy, and male stigma as it affects men's identity.

He is currently President of the *New Enlightenment Project: A Canadian Humanist Initiative*.

Teela Robertson, MC. is a psychologist in Alberta who started in a not-for-profit as a community clinical counsellor. She moved into private practice in 2020 with a focus on treating individual adults and couples with relationship struggles, depression, anxiety, trauma, and specializes in working with Indigenous peoples. Teela has applied Dr. Robertson's mapping to adults experiencing mood disruptions and those experiencing uncertainty of self. She approaches therapy through a cross-cultural lense with a focus on fostering empowerment and self-guided changes.

Cover design by Lianne Torres Barraquio, 2025

www.ingramcontent.com/pod-product-compliance
Lightning Source LLC
Chambersburg PA
CBHW081200020426
42333CB00020B/2572